E-LEARNING
Uncovered ℠

Articulate ©
Storyline ©

Diane Elkins

Desirée Pinder

E-Learning Uncovered: Articulate Storyline By Diane Elkins and Desirée Pinder

Trademarks

Articulate, Articulate Storyline, and Storyline are registered trademarks or trademarks of Articulate Global, Inc., and its subsidiaries and/or affiliates in the United States.

Other product and company names mentioned herein may be trademarks of their respective owners.

Use of trademarks or product names is not intended to convey endorsement or affiliation in this book.

Warning and Disclaimer

The information provided is on an "as is" basis. Every effort has been made to make this book as complete and as accurate as possible, but no warranty or fitness is implied. The authors and the publisher shall have neither liability nor responsibility to any person or entity with respect to any loss or damages arising from the information contained in this book.

Table of Contents

Table of Contents

Table of Contents

Table of Contents

Introduction

Back in the day, e-learning courses were made by "the man behind the curtain." Secret programmers with special, secret skills worked behind closed doors to build courseware designed by us mere mortals. Once it was made, even changing a comma required special skills. A lot has changed since then.

Storyline is proof that you can create a course that's visually rich, highly interactive, and customized to meet your instructional needs. They make the hard stuff easy.

- Want a way to let the students know which buttons they have and haven't clicked? Easy.

- Want to set up branching based on student answers? Easy.

- Want to manage graphics, audio, video, and screen simulations all in one tool? Easy.

- Want to use templates for simple questions and interactions, but then go "under the hood" to customize how they work? Easy.

- Want to create a drag-and-drop activity in less than 5 minute? Easy.

The creative side of me loves what I can do with it. The pragmatic side of me loves how quickly I can produce something—and how quickly I can change it.

We certainly hope you enjoy learning how to use Storyline with this book. But even more, we hope you have fun creating great courses in Storyline.

Acknowledgments

Desirée and I would like to extend our special thanks to some of the many people who made this book possible. We'd like to thank our extended production team of Leslie Harrison and Lucie Haskins. Arlyn Asch and Jeanette Brooks provided invaluable technical support to help us chase down many of the details. Thanks to Elaine Biech for lending insight on how to get a quality book out in a short period of time. And as always, special thanks goes to my husband, Steve Elkins, who helped me stay focused and motivated, kept me well-fed during the big deadlines, and found more than his share of missing commas.

Diane Elkins

Getting the Most Out of This Book

This book assumes you are a functional user of Windows software. If you are familiar with how to use dialog boxes, drop-down menus, and other standard Windows conventions, then you'll be fine.

Use the detailed table of contents and comprehensive index to help you find what you are looking for. In addition to procedures, look for all the hints, tips, and cautions that can help you save time, avoid problems, and make your courses more engaging.

 DESIGN TIP

Design Tips give you insight on how to implement the different features and include everything from graphic design to instructional design to usability.

 CAUTION

Pay special attention to the Cautions (which are full of "lessons learned the hard way") so you can avoid some common problems.

 BRIGHT IDEA

Bright Ideas are special explanations and ideas for getting more out of the software.

 POWER TIP

Power Tips are advanced tips and secrets that can help you take your production to the next level.

 TIME SAVER

Time Savers...well...save you time. These tips include software shortcuts and ways to streamline your production efforts.

 This symbol indicates a cross-reference to another part of the book.

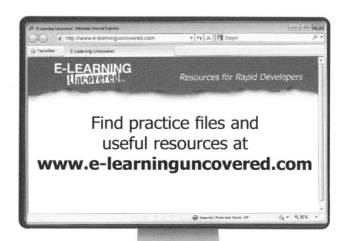

Find practice files and useful resources at **www.e-learninguncovered.com**

Getting to Know Storyline

Introduction

Articulate Storyline is a rapid development authoring tool that lets you create engaging, interactive e-learning courses without programming knowledge. With Storyline, you can create courses with text, graphics, animations, audio, video, screen simulations, interactions, branching, and questions.

Storyline is a standalone software package, yet it integrates well with content you might already have in Microsoft PowerPoint, Articulate Engage, or Articulate Quizmaker. The interface and features are designed for the non-programmer and take advantage of many of the things you probably already know how to do in PowerPoint.

When your course is complete, you will have a number of output options. You can publish to Flash or HTML5 output to view on web pages, CD-ROMs, learning management systems, or mobile devices.

In This Chapter

- Stories, Scenes, and Pages
- Story View
- Slide View
- View Options
- Opening a Project
- Previewing a Project

Notes

Stories, Scenes, and Pages

A Storyline project is made up of slides, organized into scenes, that make up a story. Think of it as pages (slides) in a chapter (scene) in a book (story). The story contains all the content for a single course. You'll learn how to set up new story projects in chapter 2 and how to work with scenes and pages in chapter 3.

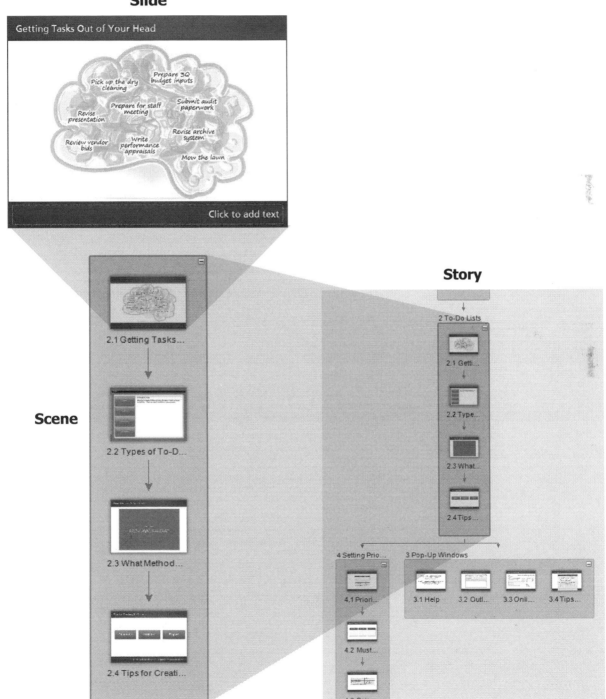

Story View

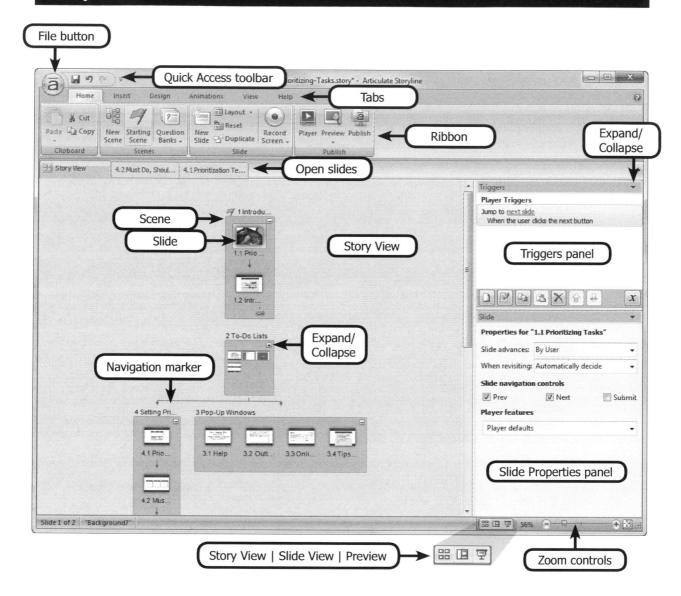

Working In Story View

- Select a slide to view its information in the panes on the right.
- Double-click a slide to open it.
- Click the **Expand/Collapse** icon to make scenes bigger or smaller.
- Click the tabs just below the ribbon to move from **Story View** to **Slide View** of open slides.

Slide View

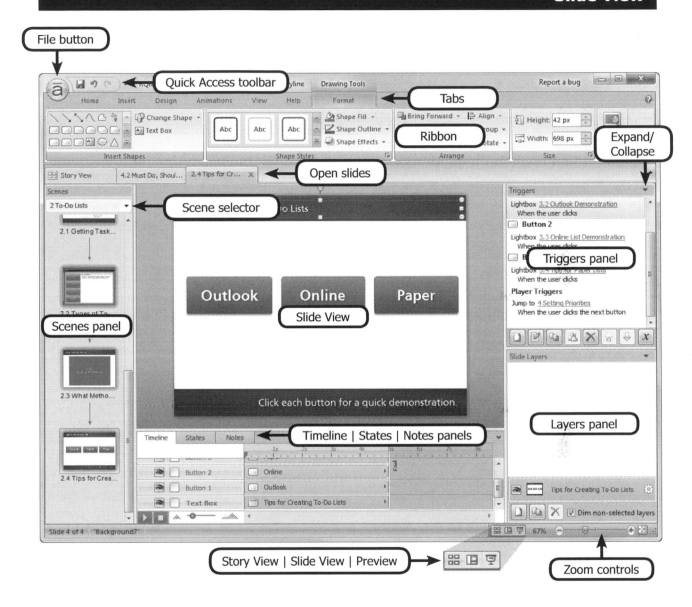

File button

Quick Access toolbar

Tabs

Ribbon

Expand/Collapse

Open slides

Scene selector

Triggers panel

Scenes panel

Slide View

Timeline | States | Notes panels

Layers panel

Story View | Slide View | Preview

Zoom controls

Working In Slide View

- Click the **X** on a tab to close that slide.
- Click a thumbnail in the **Scenes** panel to open a different slide in the current tab.
- Click the scene selector drop-down menu to select a different scene to view in the panel.

View Options

In addition to the elements featured on the previous pages, use the **View** tab to customize your view.

Story View/Normal: Use these buttons as one way to switch between **Story View** and **Page View** (normal).

Slide Master: Use this button to create or edit slide masters, which is covered in chapter 3.

Feedback Master: Use this button to create or edit slide masters for question feedback, which is covered on page 168.

The following items are only available when you are in **Slide View**. They are used to help with object placement, which is covered in chapter 7.

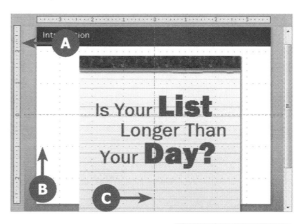

- **Ruler**: Check this box to show a ruler on the top and bottom of the slide. **(A)**

- **Gridlines**: Check this box to show a grid on the slide. **(B)**

- **Guides**: Check this box to show vertical and horizontal lines that you can position where you want them. **(C)**

 Gridlines and Guides, p. 76

Zoom: Available only in **Slide View**, click this button to get more precise control over the zoom percentage.

Fit to Window: Click this button to zoom the view so that the entire slide is visible.

Preview: Click this button to see what the course looks like. Previewing is covered on page 8.

 TIME SAVER

You can access the **Zoom** dialog box and the **Fit to Window** feature at any time using the controls at the bottom of the interface.

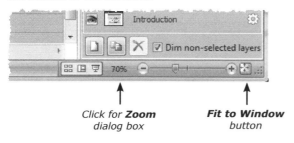

Click for **Zoom**   **Fit to Window**
dialog box   button

Open an Existing Project

To open an existing project:

1. Select the file in the **Open a Recent Project** section of the start page.

—— or ——

1. Click the **Browse** link in the bottom corner of the start page.
2. Find and select the project you want.
3. Click the **Open** button.

—— or ——

1. Click the **File** button. **(A)**
2. Select **Open**.
3. Find and select the project you want.
4. Click the **Open** button.

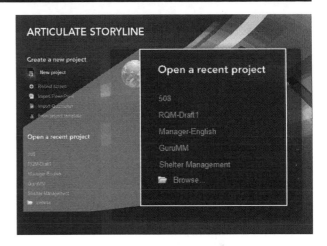

 CAUTION

If you try to open a project while you have another project open, the first project will close. If you want to have two projects open at once, launch the software twice. You can have one project open in each instance. However, you may experience slower performance with two instances open at the same time.

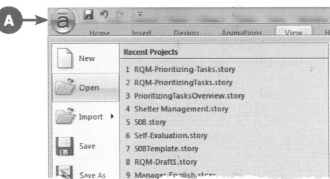

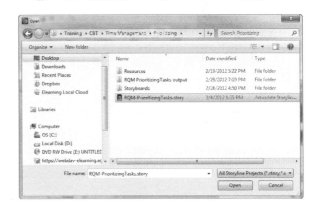

Preview a Project

You can preview a project from any tab in the software. It is usually to the far right of the ribbon.

To preview a project:

1. Click the **Preview** drop-down arrow.
2. Select **This Slide**, **This Scene**, or **Entire Project**.

 TIME SAVER

The **Preview** button is split into two parts. If you click the top part instead of the drop-down arrow, the whole project gets previewed.

Once you are in preview mode, you can use the buttons on the **Preview** ribbon to:

- Close the preview, and return to edit mode.

- Move from slide to slide by clicking the **Select** button and then selecting the slide you want to jump to. (Only slides included in the preview are available.)

- Replay either the current slide, current scene, or whole project. (The options available vary based on how much of the project you are previewing.)

- Edit the slide that is currently showing, meaning switch to **Slide View**.

 CAUTION

If you only preview part of the project, some course features may not function. For example, if you have a link to a page that isn't part of the preview, that link will not work.

Creating New Projects

Introduction

When creating new projects, you can either start from scratch with a new blank file or reuse content by creating a new project from PowerPoint, Articulate Presenter, or a template. Even if you start with a blank project, you can still import slides later, which you'll learn about in chapter 3. You can also create a new project by recording your screen, which you'll learn about in chapter 13.

Also in this chapter, you'll learn how to set the size of the slides in your project and save it, either as a regular file or as a template.

In This Chapter

- Blank Projects
- Projects From PowerPoint
- Projects From Quizmaker
- Projects From a Template
- Changing Story Size
- Saving Projects

Notes

Create a New Blank Project

To create a new blank project:

1. Click the **File** button.
2. Select **New**.

———— or ————

1. Click **New Project** on the start page.

Importing From PowerPoint

If you already have slides built in PowerPoint, you can create a new Storyline project from them. In chapter 3, you'll learn how to import PowerPoint slides into an existing project.

When you import individual PowerPoint slides, you can still edit them. Rather than appear as a single image or Flash file, the slides are brought in with the images, text, slide notes, and other elements in tact. This means you can edit and modify them in Storyline.

Many of the features of your PowerPoint slides will appear on your Storyline slides exactly as they appeared in PowerPoint. However, some features may not. For example, some animations, text effects, and graphic effects may not be available in Storyline. In these cases, those effects are substituted for something that is available in Storyline. Audio that was recorded on the slide in PowerPoint or added in Articulate presenter will be imported; however, audio attached as a file in PowerPoint will not.

Be sure to check your newly imported slides in Storyline to see how the slides are being interpreted.

Create a New Project From PowerPoint

To create a new project from a PowerPoint file:

1. Click **Import PowerPoint** on the start page.
2. Find and select the file you want to import.
3. Click the **Open** button.
4. In the **Insert Slides** dialog box, select the slides you want to import.
5. Click the **Import** button.

Use the following features in the **Insert Slides** dialog box to help streamline the import process.

- Click a slide to select or deselect it.
- Click the **Select All** or **None** links in the top right corner to select or deselect all the slides at once.
- Click the browse button (...) to change the file to import from.
- In the **Scene** field at the bottom, select the scene where you want the slides inserted.

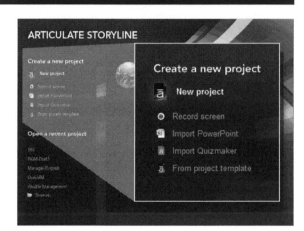

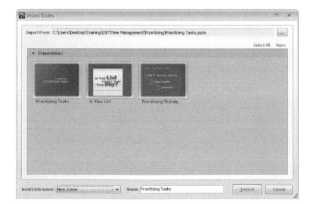

Importing From Quizmaker

If you have quizzes built in Articulate Quizmaker, you can import them into Storyline. Why might you want to?

- You may have content in Quizmaker that you want to incorporate into a larger Storyline course.
- You have subject-matter experts who have and know how to use Quizmaker, so they can help put together part of your Storyline course.
- It may be possible to build many of your questions with the templates available in Quizmaker, but you want to bring them into Storyline to use some of the custom question options available.

If you have the Quizmaker source files (**.quiz**), you can create a new project based on them. In chapter 3, you'll learn how to import Quizmaker slides into an existing Storyline project.

Create a New Project From Quizmaker

To create a new project from a Quizmaker file:

1. Click **Import Quizmaker** on the start page.
2. Find and select the file you want to import.
3. Click the **Open** button.
4. Select the **Quizmaker** slides you want to import.
5. Click the **Import** button.

Select the slides and enter the name for the scene the same way for Quizmaker slides as you would for PowerPoint slides, as described on the previous page.

 Questions and Quizzes, ch. 12

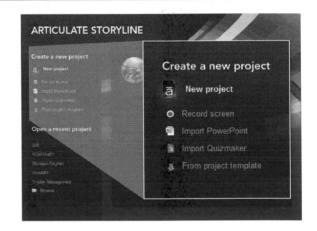

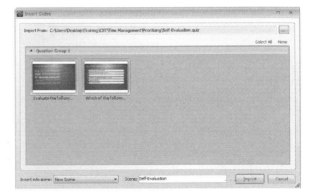

Create a New Project From a Template

If you save a Storyline project as a template, all content, logic, and settings are saved to the template. When you create a new project from that template, it opens the Storyline project as a new file, and you can select which slides to include or exclude.

 Save a Project, p. 16

To create a new project from a template:
1. Click **From project template** on the start page.
2. Find and select the template you want to work with.
3. Click the **Open** button.
4. Select the slides you want to include in your new file.
5. In the drop-down menu in the bottom left, indicate if you want to import the selected slides using the same scene structure as the template or all in one new scene.
6. Click the **Import** button.

 CAUTION

Don't confuse opening the template with creating a new file from the template. If you use the **Open** command, you will open the **.storytemplate** file and any changes will be made to the template itself. But if you use the **From project template** command, you are creating a new **.story** file based on that template, leaving the original template untouched.

BRIGHT IDEA

Useful File Extensions

.story = Storyline project file

.storytemplate = Storyline template file

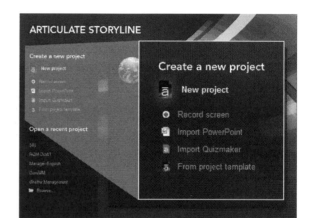

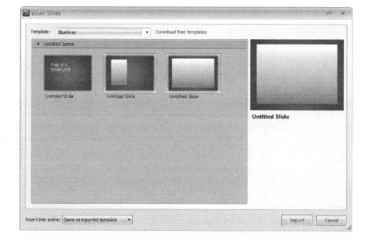

Change Story Size

When you create a new, blank project, the default size is 720 x 540 pixels (which is the same size as a PowerPoint slide), but you can change the size if you want to.

To change story size:

1. Go to the **Design** tab.
2. Click the **Story Size** button.
3. Select a pre-set size from the drop-down menu or enter your own pixel dimensions.
4. Set the options for larger vs. smaller projects.
5. Click the **OK** button.

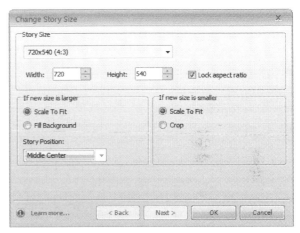

Sizing Options

Lock Aspect Ratio

Check this box to keep the current proportion of the slides. With this box checked, you only have to enter one of the dimensions, and the other will populate accordingly.

If New Size Is Larger

Scale To Fit: Select this option if you want to enlarge the entire slide to fit in the new size. Objects on the slide will resize accordingly.

Fill Background: Select this option if you want to keep the background and objects at their current sizes, meaning the project will be bigger than the slide content. If you select this option, use the **Story Position** drop-down menu to indicate where in the larger window you want the content to appear (center, top left, etc.).

If New Size Is Smaller

Scale To Fit: Select this option if you want to scale down the slides and objects to fit in the new size.

Crop: Select this option if you want to keep the background and objects at their current sizes, meaning the project will be smaller than the content, cutting part of it off. If you select this option, the **Next** button becomes active, letting you indicate what part to keep and what part to crop, either on a slide-by-slide basis or for the whole project.

 CAUTION

It is always best to designate the project size before you get started with your design, to avoid size conflicts later.

Always check your work after resizing. When reducing size, text might become too small to read. When enlarging, some graphics might become fuzzy.

 DESIGN TIP

When deciding on your story size, consider the player as well. The default story size of 720 x 540 pixels plus the default player configuration comes out to 979 x 656 pixels.

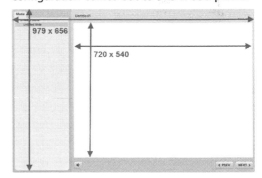

 Player, ch. 14

Save a Project

As with most software, you can save the file with either a **Save** command or a **Save As** command. If you have a file that has already been saved at least once, you can use the **Save** command to save the file in the same location with the same name. Use the **Save As** command to save it in a new location and/or with a new name.

If the file has not previously been saved, it does not matter which option you use—you will be asked for a name and location regardless.

To save a project using the Save command:

1. Click the **Save** button on the **Quick Access** toolbar.

——— or ———

1. Click the **File** button.
2. Select **Save**.

To save a project using the Save As command:

1. Click the **File** button.
2. Select **Save as**.
3. Navigate to the folder where you want to save the project.
4. In the **File** name field, type a name for the project.
5. Click **Save**.

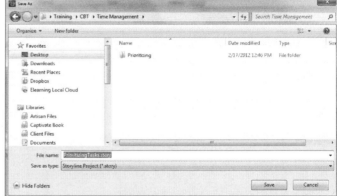

 TIME SAVER

You can also save your project as a template, making it easier to reuse elements on future projects. To save a project as a template, select **Storyline Template** from the **Save as type** drop-down menu.

 Create a New Project From a Template, p. 14

 CAUTION

It is best not to save your project on a network or USB drive. Instead, save it to your local drive.

Scenes and Slides

Introduction

Your slides are the backbone of your project. As you read in chapter 1, these slides can be organized into scenes. In this chapter, you'll learn how and why to organize your slides into scenes.

Then in chapter 2, you learned some ways to create a new project by importing slides. In this chapter, you'll learn to use a similar process to import individual slides into an existing project.

You'll also learn how to manage your slides by deleting, cutting, copying, pasting, duplicating, and rearranging them.

To help save time and achieve a consistent look-and-feel, you can set up slide themes that include formatting elements and slide masters which include specific layouts, content, and content placeholders.

Finally, you'll learn about various slide features and properties such as navigation and slide notes.

In addition to what you'll learn in this chapter, you can learn about question slides in chapter 12 and recording slides in chapter 13.

In This Chapter

- Scenes
- Opening and Closing Slides
- Adding New Slides
- Managing Slides
- Slide Themes
- Slide Masters
- Slide Transitions
- Slide Notes
- Basic Slide Navigation
- Slide Properties

Notes

What Are Scenes?

Scenes are groupings of slides. Why create scenes? Primarily, the goal of scenes is to help organize your content, either for your benefit or for your students' benefit.

- If you include a menu in your course, each scene becomes a first-level item in the outline with its slides becoming second-level items in the outline.

 Menus, p. 208

- If you have a large course, you can expand and collapse individual scenes in **Story View**, making it easier to find what you want.
- When you have to select a slide from a drop-down menu (such as when hyperlinking to a slide), having them organized into scenes can make it easier to find what you want.
- You might have a section of content that you want to reuse in another course. Having it all together in a scene can make it easier to import.

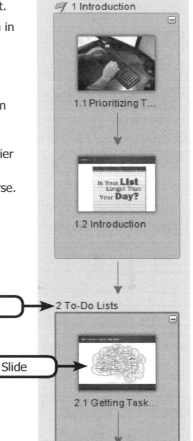

Menu in published course

Story View

Add a New Scene

To add a new scene:

1. In **Story View**, click the **New Scene** button.

New scenes automatically have one slide added to them.

Managing Scenes in Story View

To select a scene:

1. Click anywhere in the gray background of a scene.

To expand/collapse a scene:

1. Click the **Expand/Collapse** icon. **(A)**

——— or ———

1. Right-click in a scene.
2. Select **Collapse all scenes**.

To delete a scene:

1. Right-click the scene.
2. Select **Delete**.

To change the name of a scene:

1. Double-click the name of the scene.
2. Type a new name.

To indicate which scene is used as the start of the course:

1. Right-click the scene.
2. Select **Starting Scene**.

——— or ———

1. Select the scene.
2. Click the **Set as Starting** button on the **Home** tab.

A green flag **(B)** is your visual indicator as to which scene is the starting scene.

To cut, copy, paste, or duplicate a scene:

1. Right-click the scene.
2. Select **Cut**, **Copy**, **Paste**, or **Duplicate**.

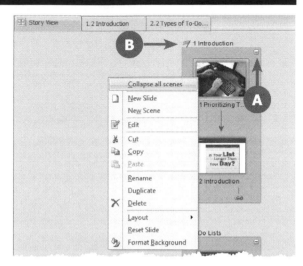

Open an Existing Slide

You can use either of the following methods to open an existing slide from **Story View** to edit in **Slide View**. Each slide opens in its own tab.

- Double-click the slide.
- Right-click the slide, and select **Edit**.

If you are already in **Slide View**, change the open slide by selecting a thumbnail in the **Scenes** panel. **(A)** This replaces whatever slide is open on the current tab.

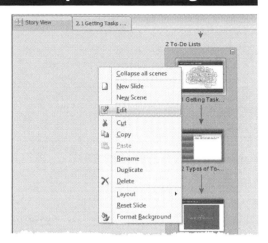

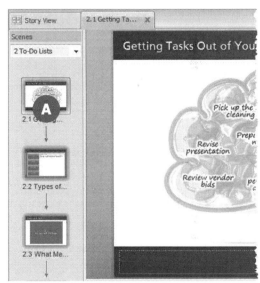

Close an Open Slide

To close an open slide, click the **X** in the tab for that slide. **(B)**

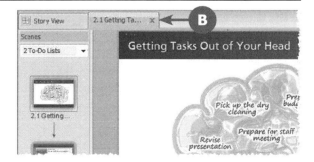

Add a New Blank Slide

Adding a new blank slide in Storyline is very much like adding a new blank slide in PowerPoint. You can choose from different master slides that can include different screen layouts and design themes.

 Slide Masters, p. 31

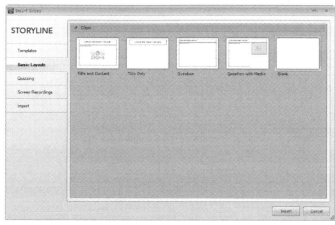

To add a new blank slide:

1. Go to the **Home** tab.
2. Click the **New Slide** button.
3. Click the **Basic Layouts** tab.
4. Select the slide layout you want.
5. Click the **Insert** button.

 BRIGHT IDEA

If you first select a slide in **Story View** or the **Scenes** panel, your new slide is inserted after the existing slide.

Add a New Slide From a Template

Just as you can create a new project from a template, you can add individual slides from templates.

To add a slide from a template:

1. Go to the **Home** tab.
2. Click the **New Slide** button.
3. Click the **Templates** tab.
4. In the **Template** drop-down menu at the top, select the template you want to pull from.
5. Select the slide or slides you want to import.
6. In the drop-down menu at the bottom, indicate if you want the new slides to appear in the current scene, use the same structure as the template, or in a new scene.
7. Click the **Import** button.

 TIME SAVERS

- You can download free templates from the Articulate website! From the **Insert Slides** dialog box, click the **Download free templates** link to view the options.

- Select more than one slide at once using the **Shift** key (for consecutive slides), the **Ctrl** key (for non-consecutive slides), or **Ctrl + A** (for all slides).

Import a Slide

You can import slides from PowerPoint, Articulate Quizmaker, Articulate Engage, or another Storyline project.

Slides imported from PowerPoint, Quizmaker, and Storyline can be edited in Storyline. However, Engage slides cannot be edited.

 Importing From PowerPoint, p. 12
Importing From Quizmaker, p. 13

To import a slide:

1. Go to the **Home** tab.
2. Click the **New Slide** button.
3. Click the **Import** tab.
4. Select the file type you want to import.
5. Find and select the file you want.
6. Click the **Open** button.
7. Indicate the scene placement and scene name at the bottom of the dialog box.
8. Click the **Import** button.

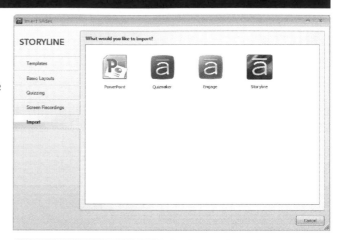

 POWER TIP

Even though you can't edit an Engage slide in Storyline, you can resize it, just as you would a photo. Resizing it lets you fit other elements on the screen, such as standard interface elements or other content.

To delete a slide:

1. Right-click the slide thumbnail.
2. Select **Delete**.

——— or ———

1. Select the slide thumbnail.
2. Press the **Delete** key on your keyboard.

 TIME SAVER

Use the **Shift** or **Ctrl** keys to select several slides at once before you cut, copy, paste, or duplicate.

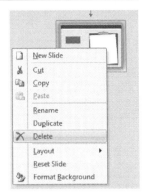

Cut, Copy, and Paste Slides

You can use the **Home** tab, the right-click menu, or keyboard shortcuts to cut, copy, paste, and duplicate slides. (Duplicating is simply copying and pasting in one action.)

Shortcuts:

- Cut: **Ctrl** + **X**
- Copy: **Ctrl** + **C**
- Paste: **Ctrl** + **V**
- Duplicate: **Ctrl** + **D**

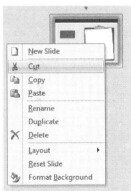

Rearrange Slides

To rearrange slides:

1. Click and drag the slide thumbnail to the location you want.

Slide Themes

Similar to PowerPoint, Storyline offers slide themes, which are sets of formatting that include background graphics, a color palette, and default fonts. You can:

- Use the existing themes that come with Storyline.
- Download themes from online sources.
- Import new themes when you import PowerPoint slides or another Storyline project.
- Create and save your own themes.

Assign an Existing Theme

To assign an existing theme:

1. Select the slide(s) you want to apply the theme to.
2. Go to the **Design** tab.
3. In the **Themes** section, select the theme you want.

Theme Options

- Click the expand icon **(A)** to show the full gallery of options.
- The top section of the gallery includes themes from any PowerPoint slides you've imported.
- Use **Browse for Themes (B)** to use a theme that has been saved. For example, you might want to share a theme from a co-worker or an online source that you've downloaded. Storyline themes have a **.anthm** extension.

 Saving Themes, p. 30

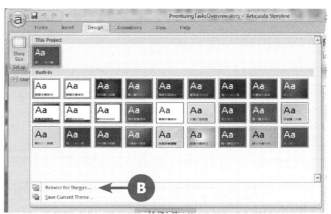

TIME SAVER

If you right-click a theme thumbnail, there are some time-saving shortcuts. For example, you can apply the theme to all the slides in the project without having to select them all first.

Change Slide Background

When you apply a theme, it generally includes some sort of background treatment, such as a fill color, image, or texture. You can change this on a slide-by-slide basis without changing the rest of the theme elements. If you want to reuse the background, you can create a new theme based on it.

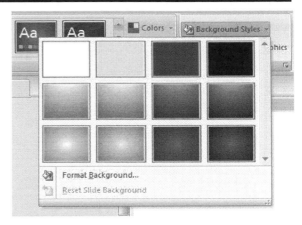

To change the slide background to a pre-set background:

1. Select the slide(s) whose background(s) you want to change.
2. Go to the **Design** tab.
3. Click the **Background Styles** drop-down menu.
4. Select the option you want from the gallery.

As with themes, you can right-click a background style to apply it to all the slides in the project.

To create your own slide background:

1. Select the slide(s) whose backgrounds you want to change.
2. Go to the **Design** tab.
3. Click the **Background Styles** drop-down menu.
4. Select **Format Background**.
5. Set up the fill option you want.
6. Click the **Close** button.

 Fill Options, p. 60

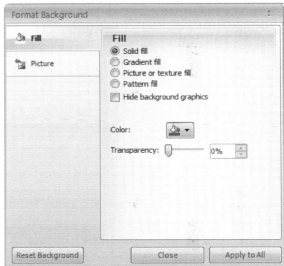

Slide Background Options

- Select **Reset Slide Background** to return to the previous background for that slide.
- Check the **Hide Background Graphics** box if you don't want to use the background graphics for a given slide, but want to keep the rest of the theme elements.
- You can also right-click a slide, and select **Format Background** to bring up the **Format Background** dialog box.

Change Theme Color

Each theme comes with a color palette that determines things like the default font or shape fill color and the colors available to you in the color galleries. When you change the theme color for a slide or project, existing on-screen elements take on the new color palette.

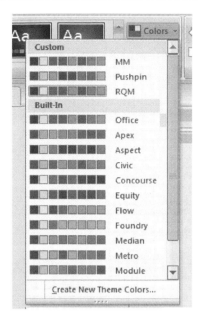

You can either use an existing color palette or create your own.

To change the theme color:

1. Select the slide(s) you want to change the colors for.
2. Go to the **Design** tab.
3. Click the **Colors** drop-down menu.
4. Select the color palette you want.

As with other theme options, you can right-click a palette to apply the theme to matching slides or all slides. (A matching slide is any slide using the same slide master.)

Create a New Theme Color Palette

To create a custom color palette:

1. Go to the **Design** tab.
2. Click the **Colors** drop-down menu.
3. Select **Create New Theme Colors**.
4. Select a color for each of the screen elements.
5. In the **Name** field, give the palette a name.
6. Click the **Save** button.

 Selecting Colors, p. 60

 # DESIGN TIPS

- The first 10 colors appear in the drop-down menu for text, fill, and outline colors. **(A)**
- **Accent 1** is the default color for shapes.
- **Control 1** is the hover color for buttons and for answer choices on quiz questions.
- **Custom 1** is the default fill for buttons.
- **Custom 2** is the default color for the checkmark or dot on checkbox or radio button styles 3 and 4.

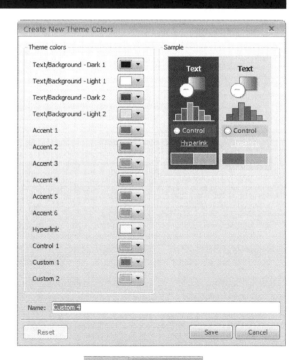

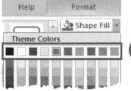

Change Theme Fonts

Each theme includes a font family that governs the default heading and body text fonts. The heading font is used in title placeholders, and body text is used with text content placeholders.

As with colors, you can change the font family used for one or more slides, or create your own font family.

To change the theme font:

1. Select the slide(s) you want to change the font for.
2. Go to the **Design** tab.
3. Click the **Fonts** drop-down menu.
4. Select the font family you want.

You can also right-click a font family to apply it to matching slides or all slides.

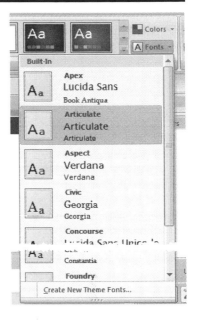

Create a New Theme Font Family

To create a new theme font family:

1. Go to the **Design** tab.
2. Click the **Fonts** drop-down menu.
3. Select **Create New Theme Fonts**.
4. Select a new font for the heading font and/or body font.
5. In the **Name** field, give the font family a name.
6. Click the **Save** button.

Save a Slide Theme

If you have customized any of the slide theme elements (background, colors, or fonts), you may want to save the new theme so that you can use it again or share it with other people. Storyline themes have an **.anthm** extension.

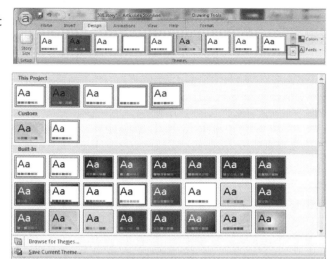

To save a slide theme:

1. Go to the **Design** tab.
2. Click the **Themes** gallery drop-down arrow.
3. Select **Save Current Theme**.
4. Enter a name for your new theme.
5. Click **Save**.

DESIGN TIP

Should you create a slide template or a slide theme? It depends! Create a theme when you are primarily concerned with the formatting of the background, colors, and fonts. Use a template when you also want to include structure, logic, and content. When you import a slide from a template, its theme comes with it.

Slide Masters

Slide masters in Storyline work much like they do in PowerPoint. Slide masters are layout options that contain media and content objects that are locked (such as a background graphic or copyright notice) and content placeholders that can be edited (such as placeholders for a heading, text, or images). Slide masters can help you save time and improve design consistency.

Any project can have more than one slide master. Each slide master can have multiple layouts based on that master. If you change the master itself, the changes are made to all the individual layouts based on that master. If you make changes to an individual layout, the changes apply only to that layout.

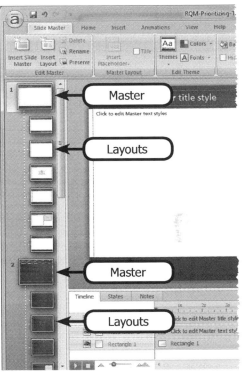

When working with slide masters in Storyline, you can:

1. Designate the master for a new slide (already covered on page "Add a New Blank Slide" on page 22).
2. Change the master on an existing slide.
3. Reset a slide back to its master on a slide after you've made changes.
4. Modify a slide master.
5. Create new slide masters (and layouts) of your own.

 ## DESIGN TIP

Remember that you can treat a Storyline slide like a blank canvas. Think beyond the normal design of heading on the top, bullets on the left, and image on the right.

Change the Master of a Slide

To change the master of a slide:

1. Right-click the slide thumbnail.
2. Select **Layout**.
3. Select the master or layout you want.

Reset the Master of a Slide

To reset the master of a slide:

1. Right-click the slide thumbnail.
2. Select **Reset Slide**.

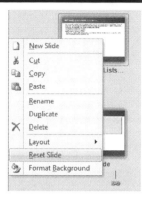

Modify a Slide Master

It is very easy to modify the elements of a slide master. For example, you might want to add a logo to the bottom corner or change the size or color of the heading font.

To modify a slide master:

1. Go to the **View** tab.
2. Click the **Slide Master** button.
3. Select the layout you want to modify.
4. Make your changes.
5. Click the **Close Master View** button.

 DESIGN TIP

- Use the **Rename** button to give your master a new name. Having a logical name makes it easier to find the one you want from the **Insert Slides** dialog box or **Layout** menu.

- Use the **Preserve** button to keep a layout with the project even if it is not in use. Otherwise it might be deleted if there aren't any slides that use it.

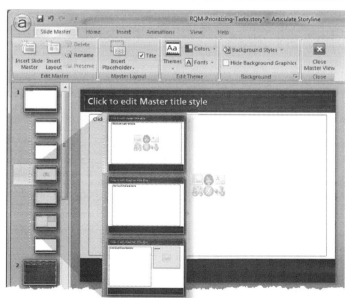

Delete Slide Masters

When you delete a layout, you delete only that layout. When you delete a master, you delete the master and all associated layouts.

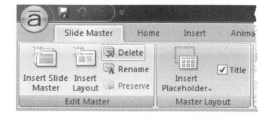

To delete a slide master or layout:

1. Select the master/layout you want to delete.
2. Click the **Delete** button on the **Slide Master** tab.

Create a New Slide Master

To create a new slide master:

1. Click the **Insert Slide Master** button.
2. Make the changes to the master (see below).
3. Make changes to the individual layouts.
4. Add or delete layouts as needed.
5. Click the **Close Master View** button.

Types of Changes

- You can make standard formatting changes, such as background and colors.
- You can add elements to appear on every slide, such as images and text.
- You can add placeholders for content that will change on every slide.
- You can modify, add, and delete individual layouts.

Insert Content Placeholders

A content placeholder lets you designate where you want text, media, or other elements to appear on a slide without actually putting any content there. When someone adds a slide based on a master with placeholders, they can then add the content themselves and know it will be properly positioned and formatted.

To add a content placeholder:

1. Select the master or layout where you want the placeholder.
2. Click the **Insert Placeholder** drop-down button.
3. Select the type of content you want to add.
4. Click on the slide to insert the placeholder.
5. Adjust the size, position, and effects for the placeholder on the slide.

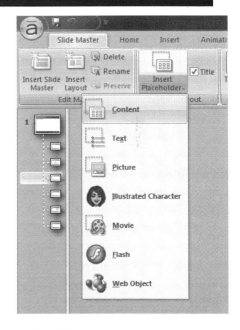

Create a New Slide Layout

To create a new layout based on an existing master:

1. Select the master you want to base the new layout on.
2. Click the **Insert Layout** button.
3. Add elements to the slide.

Slide Transitions

Slide transitions in Storyline are very similar to transitions in PowerPoint. Transitions (such as a fade or wipe) occur when the student moves from slide to slide. They are applied to the slide being *transitioned to*. For example, a transition applied to slide 2 occurs when the student goes from slide 1 to slide 2, not when going from slide 2 to slide 3.

BRIGHT IDEA

You can apply transitions in either **Story View** or **Slide View**.

Apply Slide Transitions

To apply a slide transition:

1. Select the slide you want to add the transition to.
2. Go to the **Animations** tab.
3. Select the transition you want from the gallery.
4. Click the **Speed** drop-down menu.
5. Select the speed for the transition.

Options

- To remove a transition, select **No Transition**, the first item in the gallery.
- You can select more than one slide at once when you apply transitions.
- Click the **Apply to All** button to apply the selected transitions to all slides in the project.

Slide Notes

Slide notes let you associate text with each slide. Those notes can either be used as development notes (programming instructions, open issues, etc.) or be shown to the student in the player interface (showing extra information, transcript text, etc.).

Add Slide Notes

To add slide notes:

1. Click the **Notes** tab in **Slide View**.
2. Type or paste your text.
3.

 BRIGHT IDEA

If you want to show the slide notes to your students, be sure to enable the **Notes** tab in the player.

  Player, ch. 14

If you are recording narration in Storyline, you can show your slide notes in the recording window.

  Recording Audio, p. 84

Some text formatting, such as bold and font size, show up in the **Notes** panel for the student. Other formatting, such as text color, shows up in the **Notes** tab in **Slide View**, but not in the **Notes** panel for the student.

  Working With Text, ch. 4

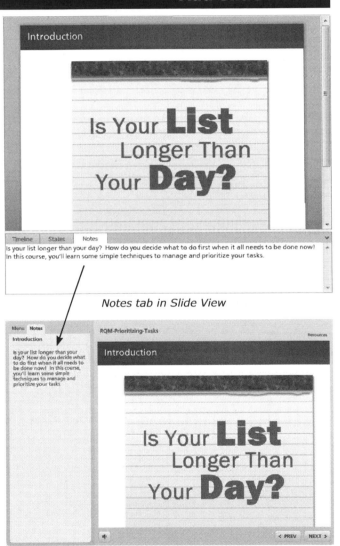

Notes tab in Slide View

Notes tab in published course

Basic Slide Navigation

When you select a slide and then insert a new one, the first slide automatically connects to the new slide via the player's **Next** button. However, slides do not automatically link from scene to scene.

If you want to set up a different order for slides or move from a slide in one scene to a slide in another scene, you can do that from the **Triggers** panel or the link icon in **Story View**. In the second half of this book, you will learn how to create more complex navigation including conditional branching.

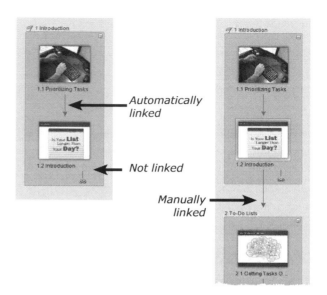

Automatically linked

Not linked

Manually linked

Change Basic Slide Navigation

To change the basic slide navigation from the Triggers panel:

1. Select the slide you want to link from (in **Story View** or **Slide View**).

2. In the **Triggers** panel, click the link for the **Player Triggers. (A)**

3. Select the slide you want to link to.

To change the basic slide navigation from the link icon in Story View:

1. Click the link icon **(B)** under the slide you want to set navigation for.

2. Select the linking option you want.

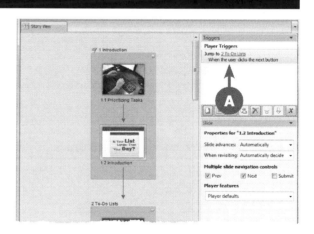

 BRIGHT IDEA

If you want to link to the beginning of another scene, it is best to link to the scene itself instead of linking to the first slide in that scene. If you link to the scene itself and then move, arrange, or delete slides in that scene, the link still goes to the beginning of the scene.

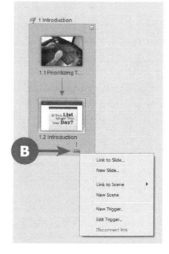

Slide Properties

In addition to the content you choose to put on a slide, you can also designate how the slide functions. This is done via slide properties. Slide properties are accessed from the **Slide** panel in **Story View** or the **Layers** panel in **Slide View**. If you select more than one slide in **Story View**, you can change the properties for all those selected slides at once.

Change Slide Properties

To change a slide's properties:

1. In **Story View**, select the slide(s) you want to modify.
2. Make changes in the **Slide** panel.

—— or ——

1. In the **Slide Layers** pane in **Slide View**, click the **Settings** button for the base layer. **(A)**
2. Make the changes in the dialog box.
3. Click the **OK** button.

Property Choices

Slide Advances

- **Automatically:** Select this option if the slide should automatically advance to the next slide when the **Timeline** ends.
- **By User:** Select this option if the slide should stop at the end of the **Timeline** and wait for the student to click **Next** (or another button).

When Revisiting

These choices govern what happens if the student leaves the slide and then returns.

- **Resume saved state**: The slide continues playing from wherever the **Timeline** was when the student left the slide.
- **Reset to initial state**: Select this option if you want the **Timeline** to play from the beginning.
- **Automatically decide:** For slides with interactive objects (such as buttons), the slide will resume where the student left off. For non-interactive slides, the slide will reset to the beginning of the **Timeline**.

Results Slide

If you are using a results slide to organize questions into a scored quiz, use this drop-down list to indicate which results slide (and therefore which quiz) the question feeds to.

Results Slides, p. 175

Slide Navigation Controls

Check or uncheck the boxes to indicate which navigational buttons should appear in the player for that slide.

Player Features

Check or uncheck the boxes for which player features to show in the player on the selected slides.

Player, ch. 14

Notes

Working With Text

Introduction

Over the next several chapters, you will learn how to add content to your slides. For those who use PowerPoint frequently, you'll find many features that are familiar to you. Storyline also has additional functions that let you include unique forms of content in your projects.

In Chapter:	Learn to Add:
4	Text
5	Graphics
8	Audio, Video, and Flash
10	Interactive Objects
12	Questions
13	Screen Recordings

In this chapter, you'll learn how to add, edit, and format text from a text placeholder, a text box you add yourself, or a shape. You'll use these same concepts when you work with text in other objects, such as buttons and questions.

In This Chapter

- Adding Text Boxes
- Editing Text
- Formatting Text
- Formatting Text Boxes

Notes

Add Text to a Text Placeholder

When you use a slide master, there may be placeholders on the slide that are already positioned and formatted properly. All you need to do is add your text.

To add text to a placeholder:

1. Click in the placeholder.
2. Start typing!

 BRIGHT IDEA

If you use a special character such as a copyright symbol, go to the **Insert** menu, and click **Symbol**.

Add a Text Box to a Slide

To add a text box to a slide:

1. Go to the **Insert** tab.
2. Click the **Text Box** button.
3. Click and drag your mouse on the slide to draw the box.
4. Start typing.

 CAUTION

If you click off the text box without typing in it, the text box will be deleted.

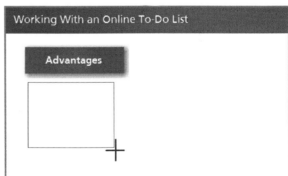

Add Text to a Shape

To add text to a shape:

1. Click on the shape.
2. Start typing.

 Adding Shapes, p. 52

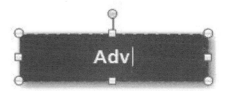

Edit Text Mode

As with PowerPoint, you can work with a text box as an object, or you can work with the text in the text box. For example, you can format the box or format the text; copy and paste the box or copy and paste certain text; delete the box or delete text in the box.

When you click a text box somewhere other than on the text (and the outline is solid) anything you do will affect the box as a whole. If you click on the text itself (and the outline becomes dotted), you are in edit text mode. Anything you do will affect whatever text you have selected.

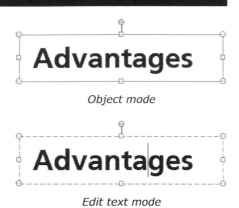

Object mode

Edit text mode

Cut, Copy, and Paste

You can cut, copy, and paste text using the following methods:

- **Home** ribbon **(A)**
- Right-click menu **(B)**
- Keyboard shortcuts:

    Cut = **Ctrl** + **X**

    Copy = **Ctrl** + **C**

    Paste = **Ctrl** + **V**

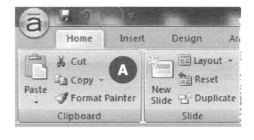

 DESIGN TIPS

- You can duplicate an object (copy and paste all in one action) by clicking the **Copy** drop-down arrow, and selecting **Duplicate**.

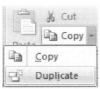

- When pasting objects from a slide with one theme to a slide with another, you can indicate if you want the pasted object to use the formatting of the destination theme (where it is being copied to) **(C)** or keep the formatting of the source theme (where it was copied from) **(D)**. Click the **Paste** drop-down arrow for these options.

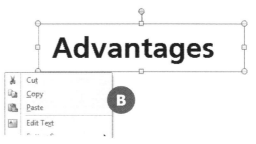

Check Spelling

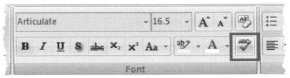

To check the spelling in your project:

1. Go to the **Home** tab.
2. Click the **Spelling** button.

From there, spell check works much like it does in most software applications.

 BRIGHT IDEAS

- Click the slide name link **(A)** to go to the slide with the misspelling.
- Click the **Options** button at the bottom left of the dialog box to change options such as the language and what types of words to exclude.
- Outside of spell check, right-click a word with a red, wavy underline to get correction options.

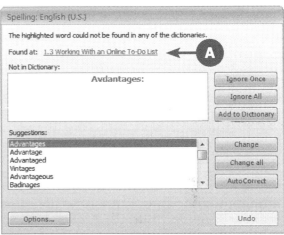

Find and Replace Text

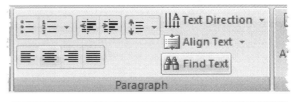

To find and replace text:

1. Go to the **Home** tab.
2. Click the **Find Text** button.

From there, the find and replace function works much like it does in most software applications.

Text Formatting Options

Most of the basic formatting options in Storyline are the same as they are for Word or PowerPoint. You can find the following options on the **Home** tab.

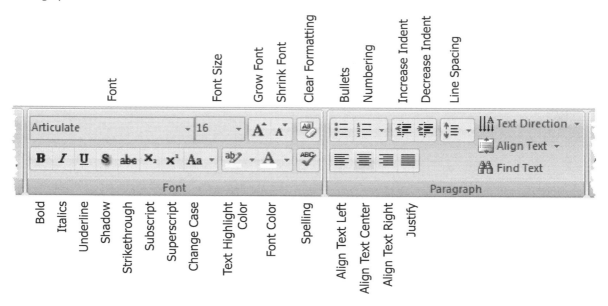

 CAUTION

- If you are copying and pasting text from PowerPoint or Word, some of the formatting may not be supported in Storyline. For example, Storyline offers line spacing of single, double, and triple spacing. If you copy text with a different line spacing, Storyline will substitute it with a supported option.

- Different web browsers may interpret text differently. If you publish to HTML, be sure to preview your project in a browser to make sure it looks the way you want it to.

 DESIGN TIPS

- Choose your font styles, sizes, and colors thoughtfully. The right combination will look professional, be easy to read, and set the mood for the course. A bad combination will look unprofessional, be illegible, cause eye strain, and cause distractions for your student.

- When in doubt, use the three-font rule: use one font for headings (under 10 words), one font for body text (over 10 words), and one font for special emphasis (under 10 words). Keep heading and body text fonts simple. However, you can have a little fun with your special emphasis font. Never sacrifice legibility for creativity!

Heading (Arial narrow bold)

Body Text (Tahoma)

Emphasis (MV Boli)

Text Box Formatting Options

In addition to formatting the text, you can also format the text box. Here are some formatting options that apply only to objects with text. You'll learn more about formatting in chapter 5.

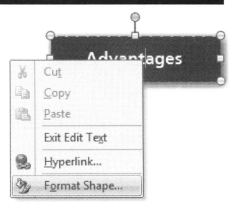

To change text box settings:

1. Right-click the text box.
2. Select **Format Shape**.
3. Click the **Text Box** tab.
4. Make the changes you want.
5. Click **Close**.

Options

Vertical Alignment: Use this menu to determine whether the text aligns to the top, middle, or bottom of the text box. This option is also available on the **Home** tab.

Text Direction: Use this menu to turn text sideways, rotating it 90 degrees left or right. This option is also on the **Home** tab.

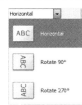

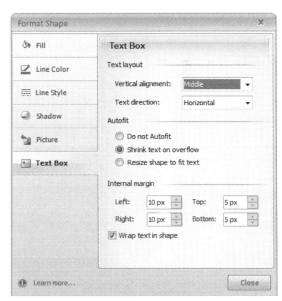

Autofit: The three autofit options govern what happens if you have more text than what fits in your text box.

- **Do not Autofit**: When you select this option, nothing resizes automatically. You have to manually resize either the text or the text box.

- **Shrink text on overflow**: This option is selected by default. The text resizes to fit in the box.

- **Resize shape to fit text**: The box resizes to fit the text.

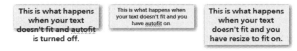

Internal Margin: Use these fields to indicate how much room to leave between the text and the edge of the box.

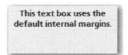 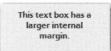

Wrap Text in Shape: This option, checked by default, inserts soft returns when the text reaches the edge of the box. If this option is turned off, your text box gets longer as you keep typing, so that the text stays all on one line.

Notes

Adding Graphics

Introduction

In this chapter, you'll learn how to add graphics to your courses, whether you already have them or need tools to create them. Specifically, you'll learn how to import images such as photos and clipart, to create custom shapes, to take screen captures, and to use the character gallery to create animated or illustrated characters.

In This Chapter

- Pictures
- Shapes
- Captions
- Screenshots
- Characters

Notes

Adding Pictures

The insert picture function in Storyline is used for photos, illustrations, clipart, and other graphics in the following formats:

.bmp	.jfif	.png
.emf	.jpe	.tif
.gfa	.jpeg	.tiff
.gif	.jpg	.wmf

DESIGN TIP

You don't have to be overly concerned with the file type you use, as long as the graphic looks good. From there, Storyline converts it to the best output format for you.

Add a Picture From a File

To add a picture from a file:

1. Go to the **Insert** tab.
2. Click the **Picture** button.
3. Find and select the image you want.
4. Click the **Open** button.

TIME SAVERS

- Use your **Shift** or **Ctrl** keys in the **Insert Picture** dialog box to select and insert more than one file at once.

- You can copy and paste images from other documents, such as PowerPoint documents.

- You can drag files from a folder directly onto a slide in your project.

Add a Picture to a Placeholder

If you inserted a slide with a content placeholder, you can add an image or other content type right from the placeholder.

To add a picture to a placeholder:

1. Click the icon for the content type you want.
2. Find and select the file you want.
3. Click the **Open** button.

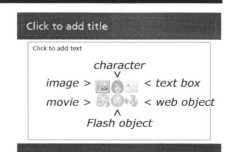

Picture Formatting and Effects

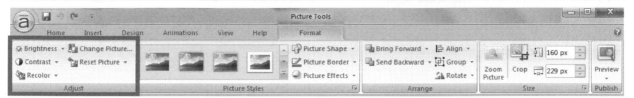

Click the **Picture Tools: Format** tab that appears when you select an image to apply special effects.

Brightness

Click the **Brightness** menu to make your image brighter (positive number) or darker (negative number).

Contrast

Click the **Contrast** menu to give your image more contrast (positive number) or less contrast (negative number).

 DESIGN TIPS

- Take brightness and contrast to extremes for artistic effects.
- Select **Picture Correction Options (A)** to enter a custom value. **(B)** You can also apply transparency to an image from this dialog box.

Recolor

Click the **Recolor** drop-down menu to change the color treatment, such as grayscale, sepia, or duotone. Click **More Variations** to select from other colors.

You can make a single color transparent, such as the white background on a photo object. Click the **Set Transparent Color** tool, and then click on the color that you want to make transparent.

Original image *Image with the white set as transparent*

Change Picture

Click the **Change Picture** button to substitute the picture without affecting other settings such as effects, animation, and timing. This feature lets you get started with your design before you have the final images, since it is easy to swap them out later.

Reset Picture

Click the **Reset Picture** button and select **Reset Picture** to remove any visual effects you've applied. Select **Reset Picture & Size** to remove visual effects and return the picture to its original size.

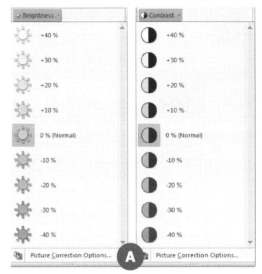

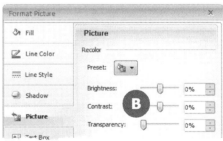

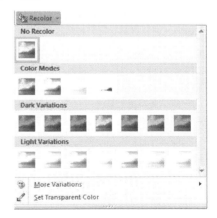

Picture Formatting & Effects (cont'd)

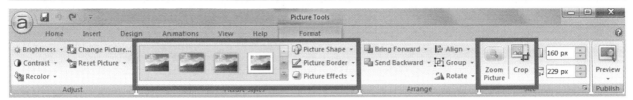

Picture Styles

Click a style thumbnail to apply that set of effects. You can then change individual properties using the drop-down menus to the right of the style gallery.

Picture Shape

Click the **Picture Shape** drop-down menu to crop your image to a shape. For example, change your picture from square to circular or to a rounded rectangle.

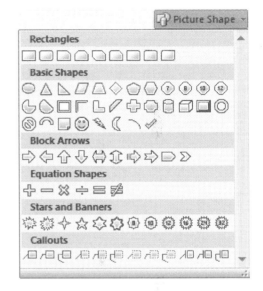

Original image   *Image changed to a circle*

Zoom Picture

Sometimes you have a picture with a lot of detail but not enough room on your slide to be able to see it well. To have the best of both worlds, put a smaller version of the image on your page, and then click the **Zoom Picture** button. This puts a magnifying glass icon on the image that the student can click to view a larger image.

Crop

Click the **Crop** tool to show crop handles. Click and drag one of the handles to crop-out part of the image.

< Crop handle

< Crop handle

< Part of image cropped out

Additional Tools

The remaining options on the **Picture Tools: Format** ribbon are available for many object types. Learn about them in chapter 6, Object Properties.

Add a Shape or Caption

To add a shape:

1. Go to the **Insert** tab.
2. Click the **Shape** or **Caption** drop-down button.
3. Select the shape type you want.
4. Click and drag your mouse to draw the shape.

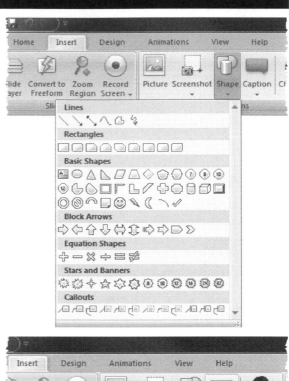

Drawing Methods

For shapes, arrows, banners, callouts, and captions, straight lines, and arrow, you click and drag your mouse from one corner to the opposite corner. The remaining three line tools work differently. In the illustrations below, the dot is the start point and asterisks are click points.

 Curve tool: Click your mouse everywhere you want a point to appear. A curved line appears between the points.

 Freeform tool: Click your mouse everywhere you want a point to appear. A straight line appears between the points. You can also click and drag the mouse to draw as with a pen.

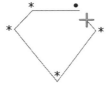

 Scribble tool: Click and drag your mouse to draw as with a pen.

Close the shapes by clicking back at the same point where you started or by double-clicking to connect the current point back to the starting point.

 DESIGN TIP

> Press the **Shift** key while drawing shapes and lines to constrain the shapes. Use it for lines to keep them perfectly straight up and down or left to right (or at a 45-degree angle). For rectangles, use **Shift** to form a perfect square. For ovals, use **Shift** to create a perfect circle.

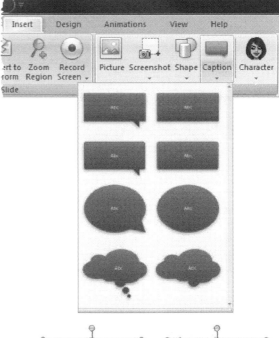

Yellow Handles

Many shapes come with a yellow handle that lets you customize one aspect of the shape such as how rounded corners are on a rounded rectangle or the direction and size of the pointer on a caption. To make the change, click and drag the yellow handle.

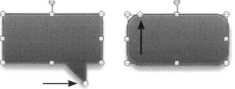

Shape Formatting and Effects

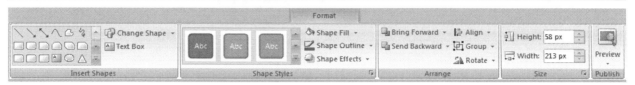

To apply special effects to a shape, select the shape, and then click the **Drawing Tools: Format** tab that appears.

Insert Shapes

Use the **Insert Shapes** gallery as an alternate way to add a new shape.

Change Shape

Click the drop-down arrow, and select a new shape for the selected object. For example, you can change a rectangle to a rounded rectangle or a 5-point star to a 7-point star.

Text Box

Click this button as an alternate way to add a text box.

Shape Styles

Click any of the style thumbnails to apply that set of effects to your shape. Once you've applied the style, you can change the individual properties using the drop-down menus to the right of the style gallery.

Additional Tools

The remaining options on the **Drawing Tools: Format** ribbon are available for many object types. Learn about them in chapter 6, Object Properties.

 **BRIGHT IDEA**

Remember that you can also add text to a shape by simply selecting it and typing.

 Add Text to a Shape, p. 41

Add a Screenshot

The **Screenshot** feature takes an image of all or part of an open window on your computer screen and inserts it on the slide as an image. Once it is on the page, you can modify it like any other image.

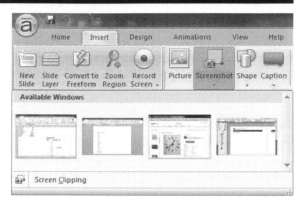

To take an image of an entire open window:

1. Go to the **Insert** tab.
2. Click the **Screenshot** button.
3. Select the window you want from the **Available Windows** menu.

To take an image of part of an open window:

1. Go to the **Insert** tab.
2. Click the **Screenshot** button.
3. Select **Screen Clipping** at the bottom of the menu.
4. Go to the window you want to capture.
5. Click and drag your mouse around the area you want to capture.

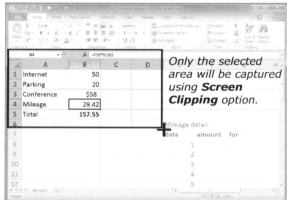

Only the selected area will be captured using **Screen Clipping** option.

 Screen Recordings, ch. 13

Characters

Storyline comes with a built-in library of illustrated and photographic characters to add to your courses. Each character comes with a variety of views, poses, expressions, and perspectives to create a custom graphic.

Here you'll learn to add a character as a static image. Once you learn about states, layers, and actions, you can create a dynamic character that changes based on what's happening in the course.

States and Layers, ch. 9
Actions, ch. 10

Illustrated character   *Photographic character*

Insert a Character

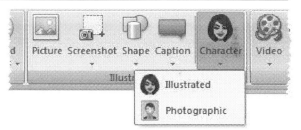

To insert a character:

1. Go to the **Insert** tab.
2. Click the **Character** button.
3. Select **Illustrated** or **Photographic**.
4. Select the character you want.
5. Click the **Expression** tab. **(A)**
6. Select the expression you want.
7. Click the **Pose** tab. **(B)**
8. Select the pose you want.
9. Click **Left**, **Front**, or **Right** to select the perspective you want. **(C)**
10. Click the **Insert** button. **(D)**

 BRIGHT IDEA

Click the **Get more characters** link **(E)** to browse for more character options that you can purchase.

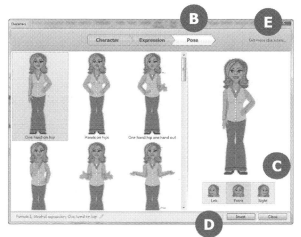

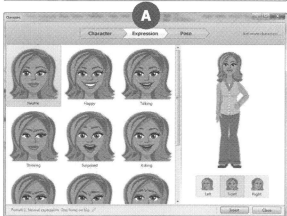

Change Character Attributes

After you've added a character to your page, you can still make changes to the character, expression, pose, and perspective. This procedure refers to making a change to a static image on the slide. To make dynamic changes based on course or student actions, you can learn about states, layers, and actions.

To change character attributes:

1. Select the character you want to change.
2. Click the **Character Tools: Design** tab.
3. Click the drop-down menu for the attribute you want to change.
4. Select the option you want.

Formatting Options

The remaining options on the **Design and Format** ribbons are the same as for most graphic types. Learn about them in chapter 6, Object Properties.

Object Properties

Introduction

You've already learned how to add text boxes and graphics such as photos, shapes, and illustrated characters. In this chapter, you'll learn about properties that apply to these objects, as well as object types that you'll learn about in later chapters (such as buttons).

In This Chapter

- Managing Objects
- Selecting Colors
- Formatting Objects
- The Timeline
- Timing Objects
- Alt Text
- Animations

Notes

Select Objects

You can select objects either in the work area or in the **Timeline**.

Slide

- Select a single object by clicking on it.
- Select multiple objects by holding the **Ctrl** or **Shift** key down while clicking on them, or by dragging your mouse around the objects.

Timeline

- Select a single object by clicking it in the **Timeline**.
- Select multiple objects by holding the **Ctrl** key down while clicking on them individually.
- Select consecutive items on the **Timeline** by clicking the first object, holding down the **Shift** key, and then clicking the last object.

TIME SAVER

Click anywhere in the work area and press **Ctrl** + **A** to select all objects on a slide.

Cut, Copy, Paste, and Duplicate Objects

You can cut, copy, and paste objects using the following methods:

- Right-click the object on the slide or the **Timeline,** and select **Cut**, **Copy**, or **Paste**.
- Select the object(s), and use the tools on the **Home** tab.
- Select the object(s), and press the keyboard shortcut.

    Cut = **Ctrl** + **X**

    Copy = **Ctrl** + **C**

    Paste = **Ctrl** + **V**

- Copy an object by pressing the **Ctrl** key while you drag it.

You can duplicate objects (copy and paste in the same action) by pressing **Ctrl** + **D** or clicking the **Copy** drop-down arrow and selecting **Duplicate**.

Delete Objects

To delete an object, select it, and press the **Delete** key on your keyboard.

Selecting Colors

Whether you are picking a fill color, border color, text color, or any other type of color, the basic color selection options are the same.

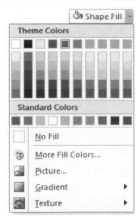

Theme and Standard Colors

The top of the color drop-down menus shows the first ten colors (with different shade options) of the selected color theme. Click on any color swatch to select that color.

 DESIGN TIP

> If you apply one of the theme colors to an object and then change the theme, the objects update to the new colors.

 Theme Colors, p. 28

More Fill Colors

More Fill Colors takes you to the **Colors** dialog box where you have several methods for selecting a color.

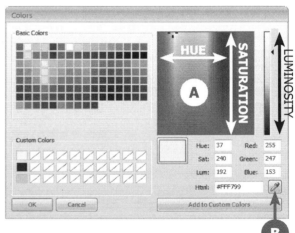

Basic Colors

Select any of the swatches in the **Basic Colors** palette.

Color Mixer (A)

Click in the color mixer area on the color you want.

- Left versus right changes the hue (blue-green versus yellow-green).
- Up versus down changes the saturation (a vibrant green versus a muted green).
- The slider to the right controls the luminosity. Up versus down makes it lighter or darker (a light muted green versus a dark muted green).

Hue/Saturation/Luminosity

If you know the numerical values for hue, saturation, and luminosity, you can enter them in their respective fields.

Red/Green/Blue (RGB)

If you know the red, green, and blue values for the color, you can enter them in their respective fields. Most organizations' marketing departments can provide their company's official color palette in RGB values.

Html

If you know the hexadecimal (6-digit) value for the color you want, you can enter it in this field.

Eyedropper (B)

If you want to match a color already on the slide, click the **Pick Color** button, and then click on the color on your slide that you want to match.

⏱ TIME SAVERS

- For colors you use often (that aren't part of the theme colors), create the color, and then click the **Add to Custom Colors** button. The color is added to the **Custom Colors** palette and saved on your computer so they can be used for future projects.

- You can make a color fully or partially transparent by right-clicking the object and selecting **Format Shape**. There is a transparency option on the **Fill** tab.

Fill Options: Gradients

Some color menus, such as fonts, only allow for a solid fill. Other palettes, such as most fill colors, give you a variety of fill options including gradient, picture, texture, or pattern.

To apply a dark or light gradient of the current color:
1. Click the color menu you are working with.
2. Select the main color for the gradient using one of the options on the previous page.
3. Click the color menu again.
4. Select **Gradient**.
5. Select the light or dark gradient you want.

To apply a preset gradient:
1. Click the color menu.
2. Select **Gradient**.
3. Select **More Gradients**. **(A)**
4. Click the **Preset colors** drop-down menu. **(B)**
5. Select the gradient pattern you want.
6. Select the gradient type you want.
7. Select the gradient direction you want.
8. Click the **Close** button.

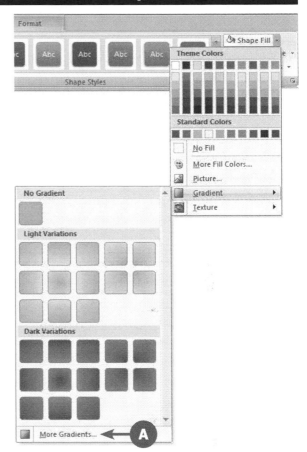

POWER TIPS

- You can also create your own custom gradient in the **Format Shapes** dialog box. Instead, use the gradient stops **(C)** to create your own gradient pattern.

- If there is certain formatting (fill, outline, effects, etc.) you expect to use the most, you can set it as the default for that object type (shape, text box, button, etc.) Format the object, right-click it, and select **Set as Default**. Then, when you add a new object of that type, it uses your default formatting.

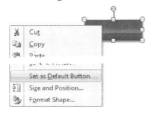

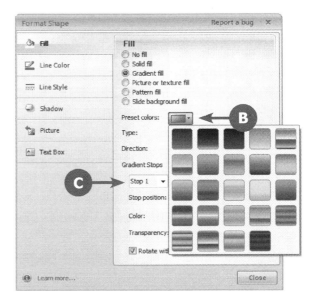

Fill Options: Picture

To fill an object with a picture:
1. Click the color menu.
2. Select **Picture**.
3. Find and select the picture you want.
4. Click the **Open** button.

 ## POWER TIP

Right-click a picture-filled object, and select **Format Shape** for advanced options such as tiling a picture to create a pattern.

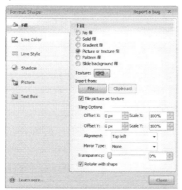

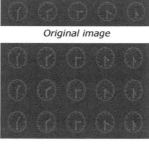

Original image

Pattern created from tiling the image

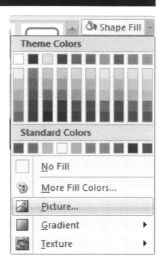

Fill Options: Texture

To fill an object with a texture:
1. Click the color menu.
2. Select **Texture**.
3. Select the texture option you want.

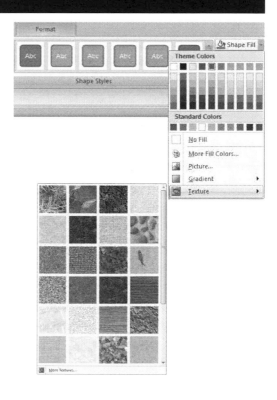

Outline Formatting

Outline formats are used for many object types, such as text boxes, pictures, shapes, buttons, lines, and arrows.

Colors

Theme, **Standard**, and **More** color options work as described on page 60.

Weight

Use the **Weight** sub-menu to select line thickness, or select **More Lines** to enter your own weight and other options such as end shape and arrow type.

Dashes

If you want a dashed line, select an option from the **Dashes** sub-menu, or select **More Lines** for additional options.

 POWER TIP

You can also right-click a line to get to the **Format Shapes** dialog box that has the advanced line options. In addition to the **Line Style** tab, use the **Line Color** tab to apply gradients or transparency to your lines.

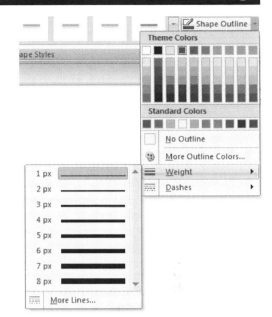

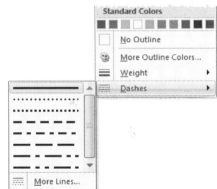

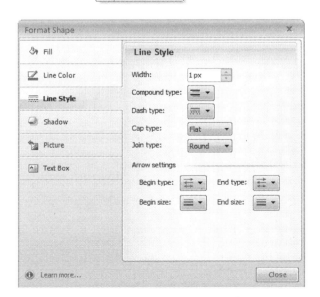

Shape Effects

Shape effects, which are also used for pictures, let you apply creative effects.

Shadow

Use the sub-menu to pick from a gallery of shadow options, or select **Shadow Options** at the bottom of the menu to create your own shadow.

Reflection

Create a reflection using the sub-menu, selecting the size of the reflection and the distance from the object.

Glow

Use the gallery to select the size and color of the glow. The color options are based on your color theme.

Soft Edges

Use these effects to create a "fuzzy" edge for your graphic.

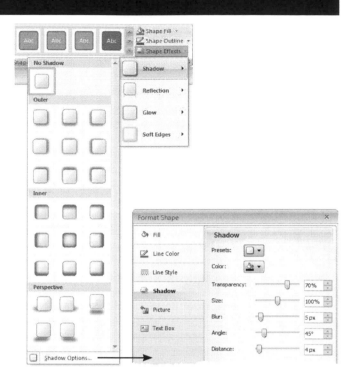

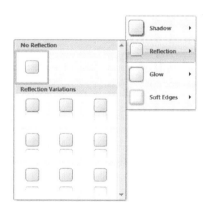

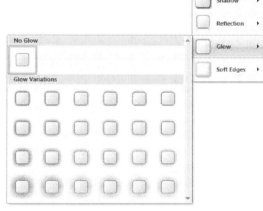

 TIME SAVER

You can copy and paste formatting from one object to another.

Select the object with the formatting you want to copy. Click the **Format Painter** button on the **Home** tab. Click the object you want to paste the formatting to.

You can also copy formatting by pressing **Shift** + **Ctrl** + **C** and paste it by pressing **Shift** + **Ctrl** + **V**.

The Timeline

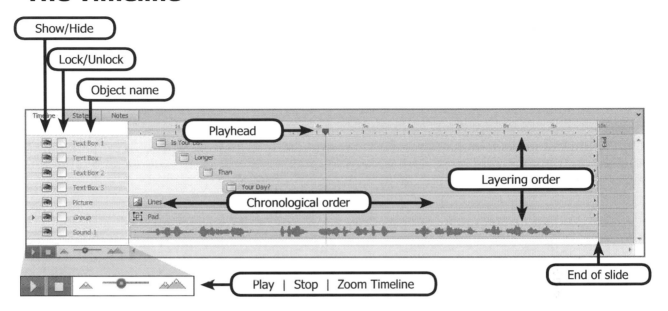

The **Timeline** panel at the bottom of the **Slide View** interface has a number of useful features. You can:

- **Select**: Select objects (covered on page 59).
- **Play**: Play the slide by clicking the **Play** button at the bottom.
- **Show/Hide**: Show or hide objects by clicking the **Show/Hide** icon for that object. Hiding unneeded objects while you work can be helpful so you can focus on what you do need.
- **Lock/Unlock**: Lock objects in place by clicking the **Lock/Unlock** icon for that object. Locking an object can help keep you from accidentally moving, deleting or changing an object. When an object is locked, you can't even select it.
- **Rename**: Change the name of an object by double-clicking the name and typing a new name.
- **Layer**: Adjust the front-to-back order of objects by dragging an object higher (bring forward) or lower (send backwards) on the **Timeline**.

 Layering, p. 78

- **Time**: Adjust the timing (start time, end time, and duration) for objects to appear on the slide (covered on the next page.)

BRIGHT IDEAS

- If you have lots of overlapping objects, it can be much easier to select them in the **Timeline** than on the slide itself.
- Giving your objects logical names helps you find what you want more easily, especially if you have to later select one from a drop-down list.
- If you are making an accessible course, the object name for graphics becomes the default alt text for that object.

 Alt text, p. 68

CAUTION

Objects that are hidden on the **Timeline** will not appear on your slide when you preview or publish.

Timing Objects

A slide plays like a movie along the **Timeline**. Once your objects are on the slide, you may want to time them to appear in the appropriate sequence and to stay on-screen for the appropriate length of time. For example, you may want to have a montage of images where each image appears as the previous one fades, or you may want to have text boxes appear in time with the audio.

On the **Timeline** for each slide, you can quickly adjust the start, duration, and finish of each slide object as well as the length of the slide as a whole.

Adjust Timing of Slide Elements

To adjust timing on the Timeline tab, do any of the following:

- Drag the left edge of an item **(A)** to adjust the start time.

- Drag the right edge of an item to adjust the end time.

- Drag the entire object to move it to a different place on the **Timeline**.

- Right-click the object in the **Timeline** and select one of the timing options.

  Align to Playhead: Click this button to start the image wherever you currently have the playhead **(B)** on the **Timeline**.

  Show Until End: "Lock" the end of the object to the end of the slide. If you change the length of the slide, the length of the object is adjusted accordingly as well.

  Show Always: "Lock" the start of the object to the start of the slide and the end of the object to the end of the slide.

  Timing: Select this option to bring up a dialog box that lets you set up the timing numerically.

- Click and drag the **End** line **(C)** to shorten or lengthen the overall slide.

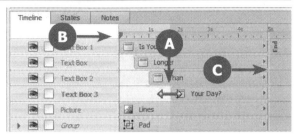

These four text boxes will appear one at a time.

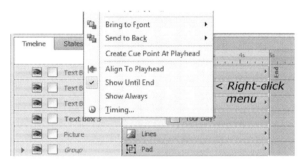

< Right-click menu

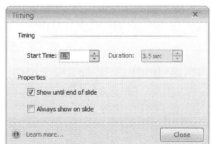

Adjust Timing With Cue Points

Cue points are markers that you place on the **Timeline** for many different reasons. The primary reason is to help you line up objects more easily. For example, if you have audio narration, you can listen to the narration and add cue points where you want objects to appear or disappear. Then you can come back and line up the objects at the cue points.

To add a cue point:
1. Click in the **Timeline** ruler to put the **Playhead** where you want the cue point to appear.
2. Right-click anywhere in the ruler on the **Timeline**.
3. Select **Create Cue Point at Playhead**.

To move a cue point:
1. Click and drag the cue point to the new location.

To delete a cue point:
1. Right-click the cue point.
2. Select **Delete Cue Point** or **Delete All Cue Points**.

To time an object to a cue point:
1. Right-click the object in the **Timeline**.
2. Select **Align to Cue Point**.
3. Select the cue point you want to align it to.

When you align an object to a cue point, it aligns the start of the object to the cue point.

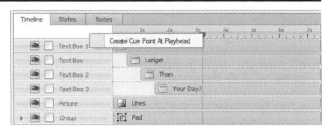

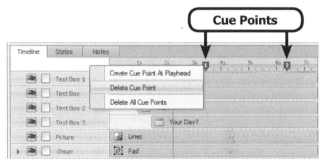

Cue Points

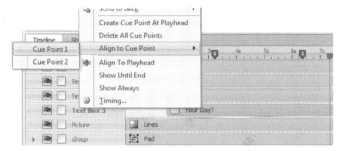

Alt Text

Alt text, or alternative text, is primarily for people needing assistive technology such as a screen reader to take your course. For students who cannot see the screen, the screen reader reads the alt text, which should describe the visual element. For an accessible course, you'll want to add descriptive alt text to any visual content. (Text boxes do not need alt text, as the text itself is read by the screen reader.)

Storyline has three options for alt text:

- **Object name**: By default, the object name in the **Timeline** is used for alt text. Changing the text here is the quickest. It works best when the description is short.

- **Detailed alt text**: When you need more than just a few words to properly describe a visual element (such as a diagram), you can enter additional text in a dialog box.

- **No alt text**: For visual elements that contain no meaningful content (such as a line separating two parts of a screen), you can turn off the alt text completely so that the screen reader can skip it.

Good option for object name >
Good option for detailed alt text >
Good option for no alt text >

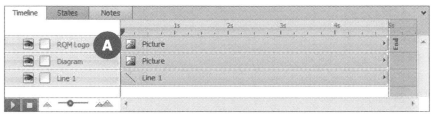

Customize Alt Text

To change the object name in the Timeline:
1. Double-click the name in the **Timeline**. **(A)**
2. Type the new name.

To add detailed alt text:
1. Right-click the object on the slide.
2. Select **Size and Position**.
3. Click the **Alt Text** tab.
4. Enter your text in the **Alternative text** field.

To turn off alt text:
1. Right-click the object on the slide.
2. Select **Size and Position**. **(B)**
3. Click the **Alt Text** tab. **(C)**
4. Uncheck the **Object is visible to accessibility tools** checkbox.

 **TIME SAVER**

You can also get to the **Size and Position** dialog box by selecting an object and then clicking **Ctrl + Shift + Enter**.

 Accessibility/Section 508, p. 243

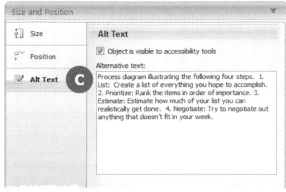

Animations

Animations in Storyline are similar in concept to animations in PowerPoint. Entrance animations play when an object appears as the **Timeline** plays. Exit animations play when an object disappears as the **Timeline** plays or when the slide is over, if the object shows for the rest of the slide. You can apply one entrance effect and one exit effect for each object.

Add an Animation

To add an animation to an object:

1. Select the object.
2. Go to the **Animations** tab.
3. Click the button for an entrance **(A)** or exit **(B)** animation.
4. Select the animation you want.
5. Click the **Speed** drop-down menu.
6. Select the speed you want.
7. Select the **Enter From** menu.
8. Select the direction for the animation.

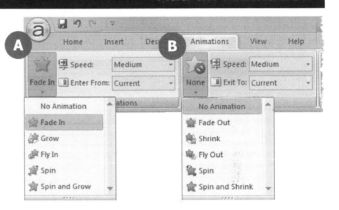

Options

- You can select more than one object at a time when you are applying animations.

- To remove an animation, select the object, click the appropriate animation button, and select **No Animation**.

Notes

Arranging Objects

Introduction

In this chapter, you'll continue to learn how to work with the properties of various objects, such as text boxes, images, and buttons. You'll focus more on how the objects are laid out on a slide, either individually or in conjunction with other objects. For example, you may need to resize an image, rotate a shape, line up three buttons evenly, or group objects to make them easier to work with.

In This Chapter

- Resizing Objects
- Rotating Objects
- Moving Objects
- Aligning Objects
- Changing Layering Order
- Grouping Objects
- Creating Scrolling Panels

Notes

Resize Objects

You can resize objects easily just by dragging one of the handles with your mouse. Here are some additional options for more precise control.

- Press the **Shift** key while dragging a *corner* handle to keep the object in proportion.

- Press the **Shift** key plus an arrow key to make the object larger (down arrow or right arrow) or smaller (up arrow or left arrow).

- On the **Format** tab, enter the specific pixel dimensions you want in the **Height** and **Width** fields.

- Select an object and press **Ctrl** + **Shift** + **Enter** to bring up the **Size and Position** dialog box, where you can scale the item using a percentage (for example, you want all screen captures to be 50% of their original size) or check the box to lock the aspect ratio of an image so that it can't be stretched out of proportion.

To match the size of other objects:

1. Select the objects you want to make the same size.
2. Go to the **Home** tab.
3. Click the **Arrange** button.
4. Select **Size**.
5. Select the resizing option you want.

When using **Make Same Width**, **Make Same Height**, or **Make Same Size**, select the object with the "target size" last.

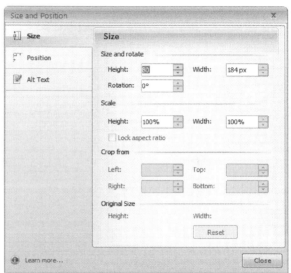

Rotate Objects

To rotate an object, select it, and then click and drag the green rotation handle. Here are some other options for more precise control:

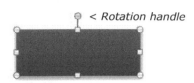
< Rotation handle

- Press the **Shift** key while rotating the object to rotate it in larger increments. This helps you be more precise if you want to have an object at an exact 90-degree or 180-degree rotation.

- Go to the **Format** ribbon, click the **Rotation** menu, and select one of the options.

- Select **More Rotation Options** from the drop-down menu to go to the **Size and Position** dialog box (see previous page) where you can enter in the degree of rotation. This is useful when you want to match the rotation of another object.

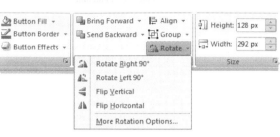

 DESIGN TIP

If you're going to make something crooked, make it crooked enough that people know you meant for it to be crooked. Something that's just a little bit crooked might look like a mistake.

Move Objects

Moving objects is quite simple—just click and drag the object, or select it and use the arrow keys on your keyboard. Here are some additional tricks that can help you place your objects more quickly and precisely:

- While dragging, press the **Shift** key to keep it on the same vertical or horizontal plane.

- While using the arrow keys, press the **Ctrl** key to move the object in smaller increments with each click.

- Use the **Size and Position** dialog box to enter the precise location using the horizontal and vertical distances from the edge or the center.

To place an object numerically:

1. Right-click the objects(s).
2. Select **Size and Position**.
3. Click the **Position** tab.
4. For each direction, select the basis point from the drop-down menu (**Top Left Corner** or **Center**).
5. For each direction, enter the number of pixels from the basis point (top left corner or center) where you want the top left corner of the object to appear.
6. Click the **Close** button.

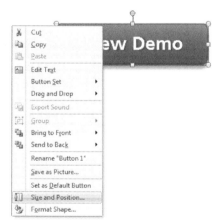

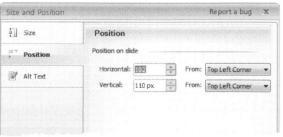

Align Objects

When you have to line up objects with each other, there are several features that can help you get it just right.

- By default, smart guides are turned on. That means when you move one object, a black dotted line appears when it is lined up with another object. Smart guides work with vertical, horizontal, and center alignment.

- You can also use the alignment drop-down menu on either the **Home** tab or the **Format** tab.

To align objects to each other from the Home tab:

1. Select the objects you want to align.
2. Go to the **Home** tab.
3. Click the **Arrange** button.
4. Select **Align**.
5. Select the alignment option you want.

To align objects to each other from the Format tab:

1. Select the objects you want to align.
2. Go to the **Format** tab.
3. Click the **Align** button.
4. Select the alignment option you want.

For left, right, top, and bottom alignment, the objects align to the object that is the farthest in that direction. For example, if you align left, all objects will align with the object that is farthest to the left.

If you prefer to align objects in relation to the slide instead of in relation to each other, select **Align to Slide** before selecting your alignment choice. For example, you might use this to center a title on a slide.

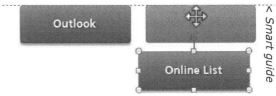

Home tab

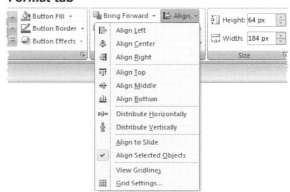

Format tab

Working With Grids

You can display a grid on your slides to help you line up items. By default, the **Snap objects to grid** feature is turned on. This means that if your object gets close to the gridline, it snaps to the grid, preventing the object from being a pixel or two off. The grid is not visible in the published course.

To show the grid:

1. Go to the **Home** tab.
2. Click the **Arrange** button.
3. Select **Align**.
4. Select **View Gridlines**.

To change grid and snap features:

1. Go to the **Home** tab.
2. Click the **Arrange** button.
3. Select **Align**.
4. Select **Grid Settings**.
5. Make the changes you want in the dialog box.
6. Click the **OK** button.

For example, use the **Spacing** field to change the distance between the gridlines or uncheck **Snap objects to grid** if you want more precise control with your mouse.

You can also access these features from the **Align** button on the **Format** tab.

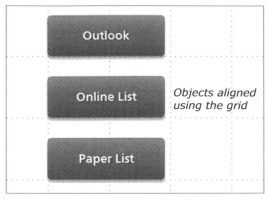

Objects aligned using the grid

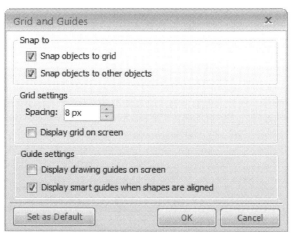

Working With Guidelines

Whereas a grid shows across the entire slide at fixed intervals, guidelines are individual lines that you add and place exactly where you want them. Just like the grid, guidelines help you line up objects and do not appear in the published course. The difference is that you place each gridline individually.

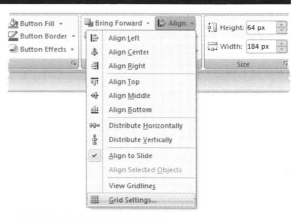

To turn on guidelines:
1. Select an on-screen object.
2. Go to the **Format** menu.
3. Click the **Align** button.
4. Select **Grid Settings**.
5. Check the **Display drawing guides on screen** box.

To move a guideline:
1. Click and drag the guideline to move it in 15-pixel increments.

——— or ———

1. Press the **Alt** key and drag the guideline to move it freely.

To remove a guideline:
1. Drag it on top of another guideline.

To add additional guidelines:
1. Press the **Ctrl** key while dragging an existing gridline to make a copy of it.

DESIGN TIP

Guidelines appear on every slide, so they are especially useful when you have certain elements that should appear in a certain place on every slide.

TIME SAVER

You can also turn grids and guides on from the **View** menu.

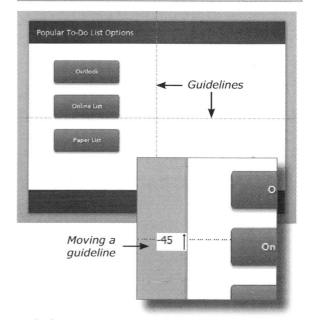

Guidelines

Moving a guideline

Distribute Objects

When you have three or more objects on a slide, you can use the distribution options to put an equal amount of space between them.

To distribute objects evenly:

1. Select the objects.
2. Go to the **Format** tab.
3. Click the **Align** button.
4. Select **Distribute Horizontally** or **Distribute Vertically**.

Change Layering Order

When you have overlapping objects on a slide, you want to make sure that the right objects are on top.

To change the layering order of objects:

1. Click and drag the object up (forward) or down (backward) on the **Timeline**.

———— or ————

1. Go to the **Home** tab.
2. Click the **Arrange** button.
3. Select the order option you want.

Order Options

- **Bring to Front**: bring the object in front of all other objects.
- **Send to Back**: send the object behind all other objects.
- **Bring Forward**: bring the object one layer forward.
- **Send Backward**: send the object one level backward.

You can access the same layering options from the **Format** tab or an object's right-click menu.

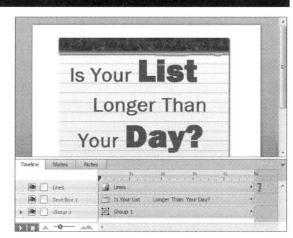

*Objects in the wrong layering order
(notepad lines on top of text)*

Group Objects

Grouping objects together provides a number of benefits:

- You can select the whole group with one click.
- You can expand and collapse the group in the **Timeline**, making it easier to manage slides with many objects.
- You can adjust the timing of all the objects in the group at once.

To group objects:

1. Select all the objects.
2. Right-click anywhere in the selected objects.
3. Select **Group**.
4. Select **Group** again.

To ungroup objects:

1. Right-click the group.
2. Select **Group**.
3. Select **Ungroup**.

To regroup objects that had been previously ungrouped:

1. Right-click any of the previously grouped objects.
2. Select **Group**.
3. Select **Regroup**.

To expand/collapse groups in the Timeline:

1. Click the gray triangle next to the group name. **(A)**

To time objects as a group:

1. Collapse the group in the **Timeline.**
2. Adjust the group's bar.

To time objects in a group individually:

1. Expand the group.
2. Adjust each object's bar.

To select an individual object in the group (to move it, resize it, etc.):

1. Expand the group in the **Timeline**.
2. Select the bar for that object.

——— or ———

1. Select the group on the slide.
2. Select the individual object.

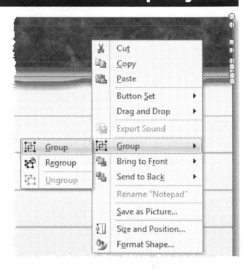

Collapsed group in the Timeline

Expanded group in the Timeline

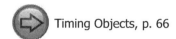

Timing Objects, p. 66

Scrolling Panels

A scrolling panel lets you add text, images, or other objects in a panel with a scrollbar down the side. For example, if you have a lot of text but don't want to take up a lot of space on your slide, you can put it in a scrolling panel. Your content objects (such as a text box and images) are created separately and then dragged into the scrolling panel.

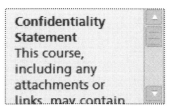

Create a Scrolling Panel

To create a scrolling panel:

1. Go to the **Insert** tab.
2. Click the **Scrolling Panel** button.
3. Click and drag your mouse on the slide to draw the panel.
4. Create your content objects.
5. Drag your content objects to the scrolling panel.

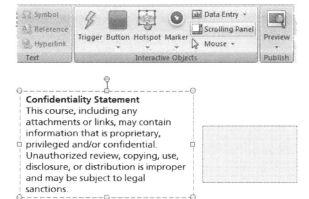

Options

- You can format the scrolling panel much like you can any other shape.

- You can select the panel to move or resize it, or you can select the object(s) inside the panel to move or resize them within the panel.

Text box to go in the scrolling panel   *Formatted scrolling panel*

 CAUTION

- When dragging an object to the panel, your mouse must be over the panel when you release the object.

- The scrollbars will not show up unless the panel is smaller than the content you've added.

Text box after being dragged into the scrolling panel

Text box selected and resized within the panel

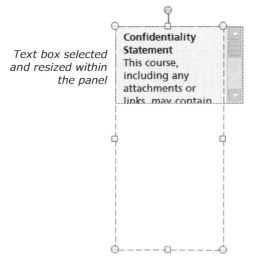

Working With Media

Introduction

You've already learned how to add text and graphics. Now it's time to learn how to add other forms of media:

- **Audio**: Import or record sound such as narration, music, or sound effects.
- **Video**: Import or record video files or embed them from popular video sharing sites such as YouTube and Vimeo.
- **Flash**: Import Flash animations or movies.
- **Web objects**: Insert live webpages that your students can interact with right in the course.

Notes

Working With Audio

You can add audio to your course either by importing an audio file you already have or by recording it directly in Storyline. You can have multiple media files on the same slide.

Audio File Types	
.aac	.aif
.aiff	.m4a
.mp3	.ogg
.wav	.wma

 POWER TIP

When you record or import audio, it is converted to **.mp3** format at 192 kbps (kilobits per second). When you publish your project, you can adjust the quality to help manage file size.

 Publish Settings, p. 224

Import Audio to a Slide

To import audio to a slide:

1. Go to the **Insert** tab.
2. Click the **Sound** button.
3. Select **Sound from File**.
4. Find and select the file you want.
5. Click the **Open** button.

 BRIGHT IDEAS

- If you import a PowerPoint slide with audio recorded in PowerPoint or Articulate Presenter, the audio is imported and works like any other audio. If the audio was attached as a file in PowerPoint, it will not be imported.

- If you import an Engage file that contains audio, that audio plays in Storyline as well; however, like the rest of the Engage interaction, it cannot be edited.

 Import a Slide, p. 24

Record Audio in Storyline

To record audio in Storyline:

1. Go to the **Insert** tab.
2. Click the **Sound** button.
3. Select **Record Mic**.
4. Click the **Record** button. **(A)**
5. Speak into your microphone.
6. Click the **Stop** button. **(B)**
7. Click the **Save** button.

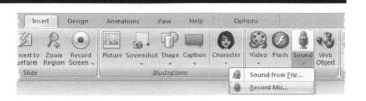

You have the following options before and after recording:

- **Narration script**: Click this button to bring up any text you have in the **Notes** panel for that slide.

 Slide Notes, p. 35

- **Import audio file**: This button works the same as the procedure on the previous page. If you have already recorded audio here, importing a new file will replace what you just recorded.

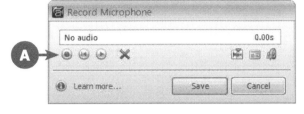

You have the following options after recording:

- **Record**: This lets you re-record the audio over what you just recorded.
- **Play/Pause/Rewind**: Use these buttons to listen to what you've recorded.
- **Delete**: Click this button to delete the audio on the slide.
- **Edit audio**: Click this button to go to the **Audio Editor**, which you'll learn about on page "The Audio Editor" on page 86.

Record/Stop Rewind Play/Pause Delete Edit audio Narration script Import audio file

Delete Audio From a Slide

To delete audio from a slide:
1. Click the audio item in the **Timeline**. **(A)**
2. Press the **Delete** key on your keyboard.

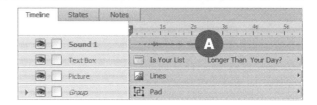

Adjust Timing of Audio

When you import or record audio on your slide, it appears at the **Playhead** in the **Timeline**. **(B)** If you want to change the starting point of the audio, simply click and drag the audio item left (earlier) or right (later) in the **Timeline**.

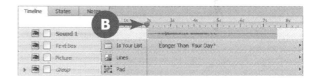

 POWER TIP

You can use action triggers to have more control over when your media plays.

 Play/Pause/Stop Media Actions, p. 125

 **BRIGHT IDEAS**

Tips for Working With Audio

The best way to get good quality audio is to start with the right recording environment.

- Use a unidirectional microphone with a foam windscreen. Unidirectional means it tries to pick up what's coming from your mouth but not what's coming from anywhere else around you. The windscreen helps reduce popping sounds from "high breath" sounds such as "p" and "f."

- To avoid echo, record in a room with soft surfaces, if possible. A carpeted room with curtains would be better than a tiled room with large glass windows.

- To reduce static and hissing, avoid interference from air conditioners, fluorescent lights, and other electronic equipment.

If you have to re-record any of your audio, try to use the same recording environment, if possible.

Don't record audio if you are congested. If you have to go back and record edits later when you are feeling better, it may be impossible to match the tone you had earlier.

If you need to edit your audio, you can use the **Audio Editor** or you can export it, edit it in third-party software, which may have more advanced editing features, and then import the new version.

If you edit your audio, be sure to check the timing of your on-screen elements. The timing may not match anymore.

The Audio Editor

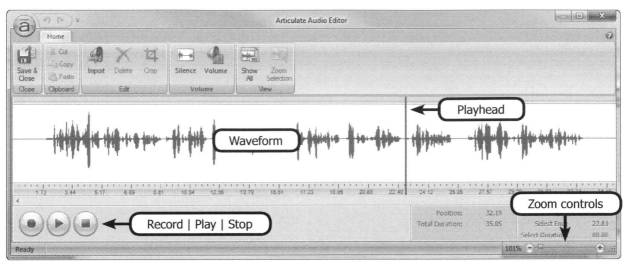

Working in the Audio Editor

- Click in the waveform to move the **Playhead**.
- Click the **Play** button to play from the point of the **Playhead**.
- Click and drag your mouse to select a section of audio.
- Click the **Show All** button to zoom the waveform to view all the audio at once.
- Click the **Zoom Selection** button to zoom in to show only the selected audio.

 **TIME SAVER**

Press the **Space** bar on your keyboard to toggle between play and pause.

Edit Audio

To edit audio:

1. Double-click the audio in the **Timeline**.
2. Make the changes you want. (See next page.)
3. Click the **Save & Close** button.

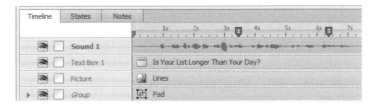

Audio Editing Options

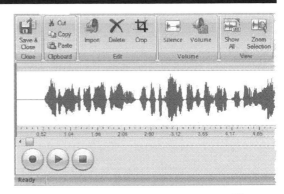

To delete a section of audio:

1. Click and drag your mouse to select the part you want to *delete*.
2. Click the **Delete** button.

———— or ————

1. Click and drag your mouse to select the part you want to *keep*.
2. Click the **Crop** button.

To adjust the volume:

1. Select the section of audio you want to change.
2. Click the **Volume** button.
3. Click and drag the slider left (softer) or right (louder).
4. Click the **OK** button.

To insert silence:

1. Click in the waveform where you want to insert silence.
2. Click the **Silence** button.
3. Enter the number of seconds you want to add.
4. Click the **OK** button.

To record new audio:

1. Click in the waveform where you want the audio to start or select the section you want the new audio to replace.
2. Click the **Record** button in the **Audio Editor**.
3. Click the **Record** button in the **Record Microphone** dialog box.
4. Speak into the microphone.
5. Click the **Stop** button.
6. Click the **Save** button.

To import new audio:

1. Click in the waveform where you want the audio to start or select the section you want the new audio to replace.
2. Click the **Import** button in the **Audio Editor**.
3. Find and select the file you want to import.
4. Click the **Open** button.

To cut or copy and paste audio:

1. Select the section you want to cut or copy.
2. Click the **Cut** or the **Copy** button.
3. Click in the waveform where you want to paste the audio, or select the section of audio you want to replace with the pasted audio.
4. Click the **Paste** button.

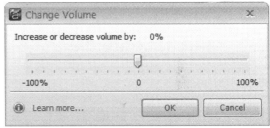

 CAUTION

Silence in a recording is often not silent because of background noise. Inserting "true" silence can make the surrounding background noise more obvious.

In these cases, don't use **Insert Silence**. Instead, copy a selection of your existing "silence," and paste it where you need some additional silence.

"Silence" from your original recording   *True silence using* **Insert Silence**

Sound Tools

The **Sound Tools: Options** tab, which is available when the audio is selected in the **Timeline**, provides some of the same options as the **Audio Editor**, along with a few additional options.

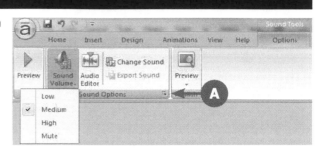

To change volume for the selected audio:

1. Click the **Sound Volume** button.
2. Select the volume level you want.

To export the selected audio:

1. Click the **Export Sound** button.
2. Navigate to where you want to save the file.
3. Enter a name for the file.
4. Click the **Save** button.

You can save the file as **.wav**, **.mp3**, or both.

To replace the current audio with a different file:

1. Click the **Change Sound** button.
2. Find and select the file you want to use.
3. Click the **Open** button.

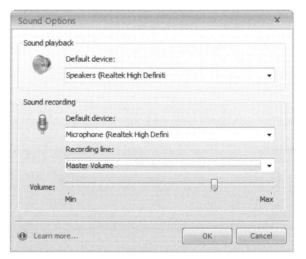

The **Sound Options** dialog box, which appears when you click the **Sound Options** dialog box launcher **(A)**, gives you options that affect the entire project.

- **Sound playback: Default device**: Select which output device you want to use to listen to the audio playback.

- **Sound recording: Default device**: Select which recording device you want to use when you record. For example, you could select your computer's built-in microphone or one that you plug in.

- **Recording line**: The recording line is for recording sounds that your computer makes. Use the volume slider to change the volume.

TIME SAVER

Double-click the speaker icon that appears to the bottom left of the slide to preview the audio. Right-click the icon to access many of the same features as are on the **Sound Tools** tab.

Working With Video

As with audio, you can either import video or record it from within Storyline (if you have a webcam or other video camera attached to your computer). In addition, you can add a video from a website such as YouTube.

Video File Types		
.3g2	.flv	.mpeg
.3gp	.m1v	.mpg
.ast	.m2v	.qt
.avi	.mov	.swf
.dv	.mpe	.wmv

Import Video to a Slide

To import video to a slide:

1. Go to the **Insert** tab.
2. Click the **Video** button.
3. Select **Video from File**.
4. Find and select the file you want.
5. Click the **Open** button.

 BRIGHT IDEAS

- If you import a PowerPoint slide that has video (added from either the PowerPoint **Insert** menu or from Articulate Presenter), the video is imported, appears on the Storyline **Timeline**, and works like any other video.

- If you import an Engage file that contains video, that video plays in Storyline as well; however, like the rest of the Engage interaction, it cannot be edited.

  Import a Slide, p. 24

- Videos can be moved and resized just like graphics can.

Record Video in Storyline

If you have a webcam or video camera attached to your computer, you can record video from within Storyline.

To record video in Storyline:

1. Go to the **Insert** tab.
2. Click the **Video** button.
3. Select **Record Webcam**.
4. Click the **Record** button.
5. Do whatever you plan to record.
6. Click the **Stop** button.
7. Click the **OK** button.

Click the **More device settings** link for the following options:

- **Video Device**: Storyline automatically searches for a webcam on your computer. If one is not found, a **No Signal** message is displayed. If this happens, use this drop-down menu to select your webcam. You can also use this menu if you want to use a different webcam than the one that was automatically selected.

- **Advanced**: This link gives you access to any webcam management software that you might have on your system. It allows you to adjust the color, brightness, contrast, special effects, etc., independent of the Storyline settings.

- **Video Size**: This menu gives you options for the pixel size of the video to be captured, based on the settings available for your camera.

- **Audio Device**: From this drop-down menu, you can select which audio device is used to record audio in conjunction with the video. In most cases, there will be an audio option for your web camera.

Add a Video From a Website

You can add video to your slides from popular video sharing websites such as YouTube, Vimeo, or any other website that provides an embed code.

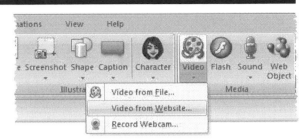

To import a video from a website:

1. Go to the webpage with the video you want to import.
2. Find and copy the embed code. (See below.)
3. In Storyline, go to the **Insert** tab.
4. Click the **Video** button.
5. Select **Video from Website**.
6. Paste the embed code in the space provided.
7. Click the **Insert** button.

 # BRIGHT IDEA

How do you find the embed code? Here are the methods for two popular video-sharing sites (at the time of publication).

YouTube

1. Click the **Share** button below the video.
2. Click the **Embed** button.
3. Copy the code that appears below the video.

Vimeo

1. Hover your mouse over the video.
2. Click the **Embed** icon.
3. Copy the embed code in the pop-up window.

Delete Video From a Slide

To delete video from a slide:

1. Click the video item in the **Timeline**.
2. Press the **Delete** key on your keyboard.

Adjust Timing of Video

When you import or record video on your slide, it appears wherever the **Playhead** is in the **Timeline**. **(A)** If you want to change the starting point of the video, simply click and drag the video item left (earlier) or right (later) in the **Timeline**.

If you shorten the length of the video in the **Timeline** (either by adjusting the start or the end time), it cuts off the end of the video. For example, if you shorten the video by two seconds, two seconds are cut off from the end.

 **POWER TIP**

You can use action triggers to have more control over when your media plays.

 Play/Pause/Stop Media Actions, p. 125

The Video Editor

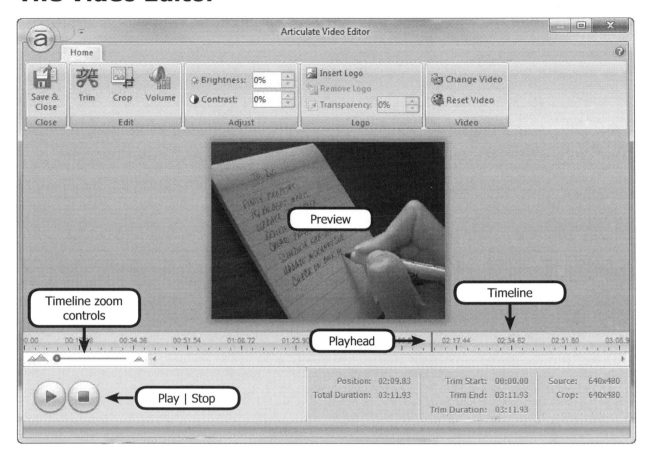

Working in the Video Editor

- Click in the **Timeline** to move the **Playhead**.
- Click the **Play** button to play from the **Playhead**.
- To fast-forward through the video, drag the red **Playhead** indicator along the **Timeline**.
- To zoom in or out of the video **Timeline**, click and drag the zoom slider. This slider does not change the size of the video. Instead, it provides more or less detail on the **Timeline**. Zoom in for very precise placement of trim points, logos, etc.

Edit Video

To edit video:

1. Select the video in the **Timeline** or on the slide.
2. Go to the **Movie Tools: Options** tab.
3. Click the **Edit Video** button.
4. Make the changes you want. (See next page.)
5. Click the **Save & Close** button.

Video Editing Options

From the **Video Editor**:

To trim off the beginning or end of the video:

1. Click the **Trim** button.
2. Click and drag the dark gray bar on the left side of the **Timeline** to where you want to begin the published video. **(A)**
3. Slide the gray bar on the right side of the **Timeline** to where you want to end the published video. **(B)**

To crop a video:

1. Click the **Crop** button.
2. Click and drag the corner handles to outline the area you want to include in your video. **(C)**
3. Click and drag the middle of the crop box to move it around.

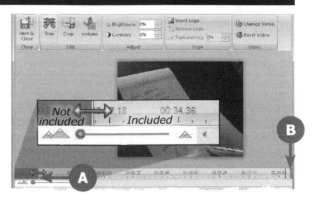

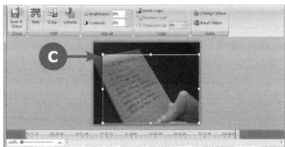

 BRIGHT IDEAS

- Your full video stays on the **Timeline**, so you can make changes to the trim or crop at any time.
- If you don't want the trim or crop after all, click the **Trim** or **Crop** button again to remove them. The settings are saved if you ever decide to activate them again.

To change the volume of the video:

1. Click the **Volume** button.
2. Click and drag the slider left (lower volume) or right (higher volume).
3. Click the **OK** button.

Note that the volume changes will only be heard when your project is published.

To change the brightness of the video:

1. In the **Brightness** field, enter a positive number (brighter) or negative number (darker) from -100 to 100.

To change the contrast of the video:

1. In the **Contrast** field, enter a positive number (more contrast) or negative number (less contrast) from -100 to 100.

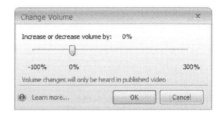

 DESIGN TIPS

- A small increase in brightness and contrast can help most "homemade" movies look sharper.
- In addition to using brightness and contrast for image correction, you can also use them for artistic effects. For example, an opening clip with full brightness and full contrast might create very interesting color effects.

Video Editing Options (cont'd)

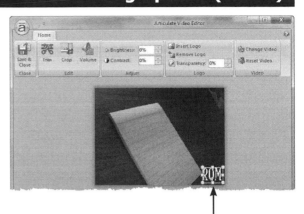

To add a logo to the video:
1. Click the **Insert Logo** button.
2. Find and select the image you want.
3. Click the **Open** button.
4. Click and drag the corner handles to resize the image.
5. Click and drag the image to reposition it.

Options

- You can remove the logo by clicking the **Remove Logo** button.
- You can create a watermarked logo by adjusting the transparency in the **Transparency** field.

To replace the current video with a new file:
1. Click the **Change Video** button.
2. Find and select the video file you want.
3. Click the **Open** button.

To reset the video to its original settings:
1. Click the **Reset Video** button.

Change Video Editor Options

To change the video editor options:
1. Click the **File** button in the video editor.
2. Click the **Options** button.
3. Make the changes you want.
4. Click the **OK** button.

Options

Enable Video Playback

If you are running into performance problems with your computer while working in the video editor, you can uncheck this box to disable video playback. You can still use the editing and publishing functions.

Clear Recently Used Videos

Click this button to remove the list of recently-used files.

Clear Saved Video Settings

Click this button to return all video settings (trim, crop, brightness, contrast, volume, logo, and transparency) to the default values.

Video Tools

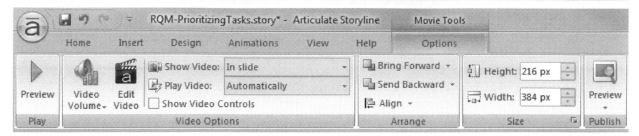

The **Video Tools: Options** tab (which is available when the video is selected) provides some of the same options as the **Audio Editor**, along with additional options.

To change volume for the video:

1. Click the **Video Volume** button.
2. Select the volume level you want.

Video Controls

By default, the video plays on the slide, starts automatically, and has no playbar or controls. You can change any of these settings on the **Options** tab.

To open the video in a new browser window:

1. Click the **Show Video** menu.
2. Select **In new browser window**.

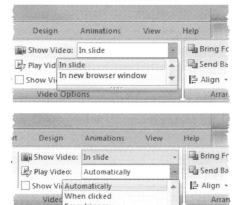

When you select this option, a thumbnail of the video stays on the slide with a small arrow button in the bottom corner. **(A)** When the student clicks the thumbnail or the button, a new browser window opens that plays the video.

To change the start trigger for the video:

1. Click the **Play Video** menu.
2. Select **When clicked** or **From trigger**.

Options

When Clicked
When the student clicks the thumbnail, the video plays. Be sure to let the students know that's what they need to do.

When you select this option, the video plays independently from the **Timeline**. The thumbnail appears when the **Timeline** reaches the video object, but does not play until the student clicks on it.

From Trigger
The video will not play until a **Play media** action is triggered.

 Play media action, p. 125

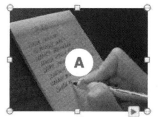 

Show Video Controls
Check this box if you want to add a control toolbar that lets the student play and pause the video. **(B)**

 POWER TIP

If you don't like the thumbnail image being used, right-click the video and select **Set Poster Frame**. This lets you pick a different image as the thumbnail.

Adding Flash Files

Flash files include an animation or interaction created in Adobe Flash or any number of other software packages that publish to Flash, such as Raptivity or Captivate. These files have an extension of **.swf**.

Once inserted, Flash files play much like video files: you can have them play automatically with the **Timeline** or use the **Options** tab to play them in a separate window, play when the student clicks them, etc. (See previous page.)

Insert a Flash File

To insert a Flash file:

1. Go to the **Insert** tab.
2. Click the **Flash** button.
3. Find and select the file you want.
4. Click the **Open** button.

Web Objects

You can use the **Web Object** feature to insert a functional webpage into your course. While a hyperlink takes the student to a webpage outside the course, a web object embeds the page into the course itself. This lets the student interact with the webpage without ever leaving the course.

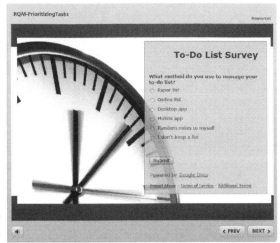

Google Docs survey embedded on a slide as a web object.

Insert a Web Object

To insert a web object:
1. Go to the **Insert** tab.
2. Click the **Web Object** button.
3. Type the web address in the **Address** field.
4. Select the options you want.
5. Click the **OK** button.

Options

Display
- **Display in slide**: This option, selected by default, embeds the webpage into the slide, as described above.
- **Display in a new browser window**: Select this option if you would rather have the webpage open in its own window.

Behavior
- **Load Web Object automatically**: If you leave this selected, the web object is active as soon as it appears on the **Timeline**. If you uncheck this option, the web object appears as a thumbnail that the student must click to activate the page.
- **Browser Controls** and **Window Size**: These options are available if you choose to display the web object in a new browser window. You can learn more about these options in chapter 10.

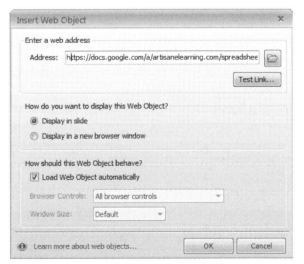

 DESIGN TIP

Displaying a web object in a new window is similar to the **Jump to URL/File** action. With a web object, the link opens when the object is reached in the **Timeline**. With the action, the link opens when the action is triggered (such as from clicking a button).

 Jump to URL/File action, p. 127

Web Object Tools

The **Web Object Tools: Options** tab (which is available when the web object is selected) provides some of the same options as when you initially set up the web object, as well as some of the arranging options available for most objects.

Preview

Click the **Preview** button to see what the live web object will look like. Click the button again to return to edit mode.

Open

Click this button to open the webpage in a new browser window.

Display and Browser

These two sections let you change the settings you made when you first inserted the web object.

Arrange and Size

Use these tools to position the web object on the slide.

 BRIGHT IDEA

If you want to change the web address for the web object, right-click the placeholder on the slide, select **Web Object**, and then select **Edit**. This takes you back to the original **Insert Web Object** dialog box.

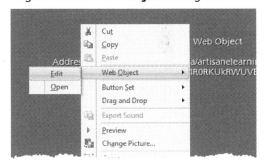

 POWER TIP

You can also use a web object to display a webpage stored locally on your computer or a shared drive, even if it isn't accessible from a network.

Instead of typing in a web address, click the **Browse** button and locate the **index.htm** or **index.html** file for the webpage you want to insert.

Notes

States & Layers

Introduction

States and layers are two building blocks that you can use to create dynamic, interactive courseware.

States are variations of an object that can be used for different purposes. For example:

- A button can have one look if it has been visited and another look if it has not.
- An animated character can have one expression if the student gets a question right and another expression if the student gets it wrong.
- A text box can say one thing when the page loads and then say something else when a student clicks a button.

Layers are basically slides on top of slides that you can show or hide when you want. For example:

- A layer with a text box can appear when a student clicks a button.
- A layer with an animated character with an audio track can appear if a certain answer is given.
- A layer with a series of timed images can appear if the student clicks a button asking for more information.

In this chapter, you'll learn how to create states and layers. In the next two chapters, you'll learn to add the triggers that cause states to change or layers to appear and disappear.

In This Chapter

- About States
- Adding New States
- Managing States
- About Layers
- Creating Layers
- Managing Layers

Notes

About States

Just about any object can have multiple states. Each state can have different formatting, different sizes, different placement, and even additional objects. You can create as many states as you want.

In chapter 10, you'll learn how to add triggers that change the state of the object. In chapter 11, you'll learn how to use the current state of an object to create if/then logic. For example, only show a **Next** button if all of the other buttons have been visited.

To work with the states of an object, click the **States** tab at the bottom of the interface.

Buttons come with these five states.

Add a New State

To add a new state:

1. Select the object you want to add states to.
2. Click the **States** tab.
3. Click the **Edit States** button. **(A)**
4. Click the **New State** button. **(B)**
5. Enter a name for the state.
6. Click the **Add** button.
7. Make your changes to the object. (See next page.)
8. Click the **Done Editing States** button.

 CAUTION

Remember to click **Done Editing States** when you are finished. Many of the software features are not available while you are in the state-editing mode.

*Text box in **Normal** state*

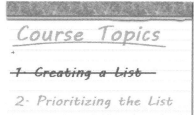

*Text box in new **Crossed Off** state with line added*

Defined State Types

When you add a new state, rather than typing in a new state name, as described on the previous page, you can also click the **State Name** drop-down arrow and select from a defined state type.

When you select one of these state types, related triggers are added automatically. For example, if you assign something as a hover state, the object will automatically change to that state when the student hovers over the object. If you set up your own state without using the pre-defined option, you would need to set up the logic that triggers the state.

For example, the **Crossed Off** state created on the previous page could have been created as the **Visited** state if you wanted the line to appear after the button launching that section had been clicked.

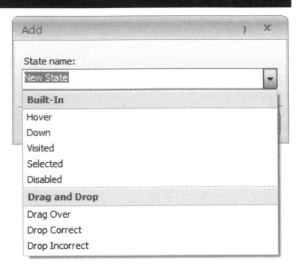

DESIGN TIPS

What kinds of changes can you make to a state?

- Change the color, such as a lighter color for a hover state.
- Add an effect, such as a glow for a hover or selected state.
- Add other objects, such as adding a check box to a button.
- Change the text in a text box, such as a correct vs. an incorrect message.
- Change the pose or expression of a character.
- Add a text box to a character.
- Change the size, such as for a magnification effect.
- Change the position, such as for an expand/ collapse effect.
- Add a sound effect.
- Combine techniques, such as adding an additional shape with an animation.

Look through all the tabs while you are in edit states mode to get ideas about what you can do. If a feature cannot be used on a state, it will be disabled.

TIME SAVER

The **Format Painter** tool works with states! If you copy and paste the formatting of an object with states, the states from the copied object get applied to the pasted object.

Format Painter, p. 64

Managing States

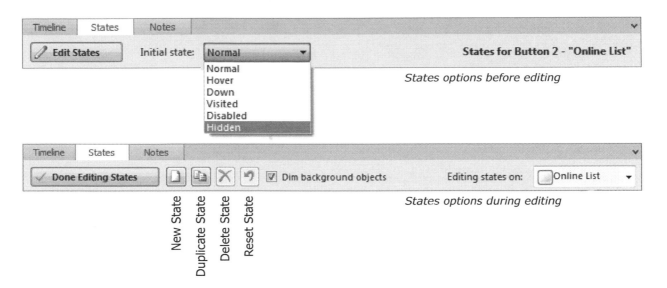

States options before editing

States options during editing

New State
Duplicate State
Delete State
Reset State

Each object with multiple states needs to have one of those states designated as the initial state. This is the state that displays if there is no logic specifying a particular state.

To designate the initial state:
1. Select the object.
2. Click the **States** tab.
3. Click the **Initial State** drop-down menu.
4. Select the state you want as the initial state.

The following procedures are all performed once you are in the **Edit States** mode.

To delete a state:
1. Select the state.
2. Click the **Delete State** button.

To duplicate a state:
1. Select the state you want to duplicate.
2. Click the **Duplicate State** button.
3. Enter a name for the new state.
4. Click the **Add** button.

To reset a state to its previously saved version:
1. Select the state.
2. Click the **Reset State** button.

 BRIGHT IDEAS

- To edit the states of a different object, select the object from the **Editing states on** drop-down menu.

- By default, all on-screen objects other than the one you are editing are dimmed, making it easier to see what is included in the object state. Uncheck the **Dim background objects** button to show all slide objects at "full strength."

- Objects also come with a **Hidden** state. It is not available for editing, but you can select it as the initial state or as an option when you use the **Change State** action type. This lets you show and hide individual objects without having to use a slide layer.

About Layers

Layers let you add objects to a slide that only appear when you want them to. For example, you could include a layer with a definition that only shows up when the student clicks a button. Layers can have multiple objects and media, and even have their own **Timeline**.

By default, layers do not appear when the slide appears. In chapter 10, you'll learn how to add triggers to show or hide the various layers.

Layers are managed in the **Slide Layers** panel on the right side of the interface.

Create and Manage Layers

To create a new layer:

1. Click the **New Layer** button.

To add objects to the layer:

1. Select the layer in the **Slide Layers** panel.
2. Add objects to the layer as you would with a regular slide.

To rename a layer:

1. Double-click the layer name in the **Slide Layers** panel.
2. Type the new name.

To duplicate the layer:

1. Select the layer.
2. Click the **Duplicate Selected Layer** button.

To delete a layer:

1. Select the layer.
2. Click the **Delete Selected Layer** button.

To show or hide layers:

1. Click the **Show/Hide** icon for that layer.

This setting only affects the development environment. It does not affect the visibility of the layer in the published project.

To change the front-to-back order of layers:

1. Click and drag a layer higher (forward) or lower (backward) in the **Slide Layers** panel.

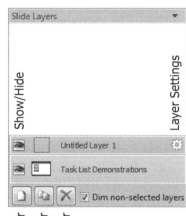

BRIGHT IDEA

By default, all layers other than the one selected are dimmed, making it easier to tell what objects are on the selected layer. Uncheck the **Dim non-selected layers** checkbox to show everything "full strength."

Change State Layers

To change slide layer properties:

1. Click the **Properties** button for the layer you want to work with. **(A)**

2. Make the changes you want.

3. Click the **OK** button.

Properties

Visibility

- **Hide other slide layers**: Checked by default, this setting means that when a layer is shown, all other visible layers (except the base layer) become hidden. Uncheck this box if you don't want the other layers to change when the selected layer appears.

- **Hide objects on base layer**: Check this box if you don't want to see any of the base layer objects while this layer is visible.

- **Hide slide layer when timeline finishes**: Check this box if you want the layer to automatically disappear when its own **Timeline** (not the base slide's **Timeline**) is done playing.

Base Layer

The base layer is the main slide.

- **Prevent the user from clicking on the base layer**: If you check this button, any interactive elements on the base layer will not be functional, but will still be visible (assuming **Hide objects on base layer** isn't selected).

- **Pause timeline of base layer**: Check this box if you want to stop the **Timeline** of the base slide while the slide layer is showing. For example, if your base slide and your layer have audio, you probably don't want them both to play at the same time.

Revisits

This drop-down menu determines what happens if the student leaves and then comes back to a slide with layers. This includes whether the slide is showing or hiding, where in the **Timeline** it starts playing, the status of any objects (such as buttons or checkboxes) on the layer, etc.

- **Automatically decide**: As with resetting a slide, layers with interactive elements resume to the saved state while non-interactive layers restart at the beginning of the layer's **Timeline**.

- **Resume saved state**: Select this option if you want the layer to retain the status of the layer when the student left the slide.

- **Resume initial state**: Select this option if you want to reset the layer to how it appeared the first time the slide played.

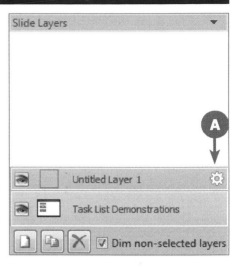

 CAUTION

You'll have to consider your slide properties when planning your layer properties. If a slide is set to resume to the initial state, all layers will resume to the initial state as well, regardless of what is selected here.

 Slide Properties, p. 37

DESIGN TIPS

What might you do with layers?

A slide layer can have just a one-word text box, or have as much content as a regular slide. Use slide layers to:

- Put in a pop-up definition that appears after the student clicks a link.
- Display different text based on what the student clicked, entered, etc.
- Show some information to a certain type of student (such as a manager) and other information to another type of student (such as a non-manager).

Slide layers cannot contain zoom regions, quiz questions, or mouse cursors.

Timed objects, states, or layers? How do you decide which to use?

To a large extent, it is up to you. There are situations in which any of the three would work. Here are some factors to consider.

Time objects to appear and disappear along the **Timeline** when:

- You only have one or two objects that appear or disappear at a time.
- The slide can have all of the objects without getting cluttered in the authoring environment.
- The appearance or disappearance of the objects is based only on time or a certain point in media, not based on student actions or conditional logic.

Use states when:

- You have relatively minor variations to make.
- You want the objects to change/appear/ disappear based on student actions.
- You'd like to add conditional logic based on the state of the object.

Use layers when:

- There are many objects that you want to have appear or disappear all at once.
- You want to take advantage of having a separate **Timeline**.
- Having all the objects on the base layer will clutter up your slide in the authoring environment and make it difficult to work.
- You want the objects to appear or disappear based on student actions.
- You'd like to add conditional logic based on the state of the object.

Triggers & Actions

CHAPTER 10

Introduction

Triggers and actions are the building blocks that you can use to create interactivity and custom features. Once you understand how these building blocks work, it is up to you and your imagination to create whatever interactions, games, and custom features you want.

A trigger is what you add to an object or page that launches an action. The action is what actually happens.

For example, you could:

- Add a trigger to a button to go to the next page.
- Add a trigger to a page that shows a layer if the student passed the test.
- Add a trigger via a text hyperlink to take a user to a webpage.
- Add a trigger to a shape that changes the state of a character.

You can "layer" actions so that several things happen on a single click (such as displaying a message, playing a sound, and adding points to a score).

In this chapter, you'll learn about the available trigger and action options that can be applied to virtually any object. Plus, you'll learn about certain objects that are specifically designed for interaction: hyperlinks, buttons, check boxes and radio buttons, hotspots, and markers.

In the next chapter, you'll learn about more advanced action options, such as how to make actions conditional.

In This Chapter

- Elements of an Action
- Event Types
- Action Types
- Adding and Managing Actions
- Hyperlinks
- Buttons, Check Boxes, and Radio Buttons
- Hotspots
- Markers
- Individual Actions
- Drag-and-Drop Interactions

Notes

Elements of an Action

Action ▸ **Target** ▸ **Event** ▸ **Object** ▸ **Condition**

The step performed when the action fires	The object that is acted upon	The event that causes the action to fire	The object that the event happens to	The special requirements for the action to run
Jump to slide	2.1	when the user clicks	button 1	every time (no condition).
Change the state of	character 1	when the user hovers over	character 1	every time (no condition).
Play	cheer.mp3	when the user clicks	the Submit button	if choices A and C are selected.

Some actions have additional fields (such as the state change shown below) and some have fewer fields.

Conditions, p. 138

Event Types

There are 14 different events that can trigger an action. The one you choose affects what options you have in the **Object** drop-down menu.

Event	Comments
User clicks	These events can be applied to just about any object visible on the slide: buttons, text boxes, shapes, images, characters, etc.
User double clicks	
User right clicks	
User clicks outside	An action with this event triggers when the student clicks anywhere BUT the target object.
Timeline starts	You can base this event on the **Timeline** of the slide as a whole, a layer, or an individual object.
Timeline ends	
Object dragged over	These events are used for drag-and-drop activities. For example, you might want a shape to glow when an object is dragged over it, and then display a message if the student drops the drag item there.
Object dropped on	
User presses a key	You indicate what keystroke combination triggers the action. You can include functional keys such as **Shift**, **Ctrl**, **Alt**, arrow keys, etc.
State	The event triggers when the state of one or more objects changes to a certain state or to anything but a certain state. (See details on the right.)
Variable changes	A variable is a saved piece of information. Learn more about variables in chapter 11.
Mouse hovered over	This event can be applied to just about any object visible on the slide.
Media completes	You can use this event to trigger an action when an audio or video file finishes playing.
Control loses focus	Actions with this even are triggered when the student clicks off of the item with the trigger, such as off of a data entry box

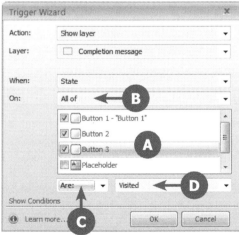

State events have several components:

- Select one object or multiple objects to consider. **(A)**
- With multiple objects, designate if all have to change or just any one of them. **(B)**
- Indicate if you want to pick a state that triggers the action (**is/are**) or the only state that doesn't trigger the action (**is not/are not**). **(C)**
- Finally, designate the state to trigger or not trigger the action. **(D)**

Action Types

There are 21 different action types. The one you choose affects what options you have for the target and if there are any other choices to be made.

Some of these actions are covered in this chapter, while others are covered in a later chapter.

Action	Brief Description	Covered on
Change state of	For an object with multiple states, designate which state to show.	page 122
Show layer	On slides with multiple layers, use these actions to show and hide them.	page 122
Hide layer		
Jump to slide	Hyperlink to other slides in your project.	page 123
Jump to scene		
Lightbox slide	Display another slide as a pop-up window on top of the slide you are on. (And then close that pop-up window.)	page 124
Close lightbox		
Play media	Control media such as an audio or video file.	page 125
Pause media		
Stop media		
Submit interaction	Grade a question made from one of the quiz templates.	page 180
Restart course	Go to the starting scene and reset everything (questions, variables, states, etc.) to the original settings.	page 126
Exit course	Close the course.	page 126
Adjust variable	Change the value of a stored piece of data.	page 134
Jump to URL/File	Go to a webpage or launch an attached document.	page 127
Send email to	Open an email in the student's default email program, addressed to the address designated.	page 128
Execute JavaScript	Add custom JavaScript code to extend the capabilities of the software.	page 128
Submit results	Process the results of a quiz.	page 180
Review results		
Reset results		
Print results		

Common

Change state of

Show layer

Hide layer

Jump to slide

Jump to scene

Lightbox slide

Close lightbox

Media

Play media

Pause media

Stop media

Interaction

Submit interaction

Course

Restart course

Exit course

More

Adjust variable

Jump to URL/File

Send email to

Execute JavaScript

Quiz

Submit results

Review results

Reset results

Print results

Adding Action Triggers

All action triggers on a slide can be found in the **Triggers** panel. They are organized into three categories:

- **Slide Triggers**: These actions trigger when the **Timeline** starts or ends.

- **Object Triggers**: These actions trigger based on the state of or an interaction with a specific object.

- **Player Triggers**: These actions are triggered when the student clicks a player button: the **Next**, **Prev**, or **Submit** buttons.

Buttons at the bottom of the **Triggers** panel let you manage the triggers.

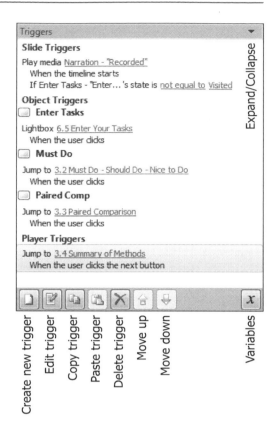

Add a New Trigger

One or more actions can be added to any object except web objects.

To add a new trigger:

1. Select the object you want to add the trigger to (optional).

2. Click the **Create New Trigger** button.

3. In the **Action** drop-down menu, select the action you want.

4. In the second menu (field name changes based on the action type chosen), select the target for the action.

5. In the **When** drop-down menu, select the event that will trigger the action.

6. In the **Object** menu, select the item to be used as the trigger.

7. Click the **OK** button.

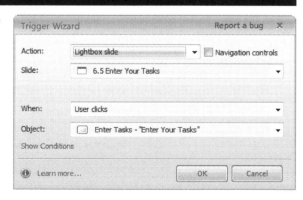

There may be additional settings based on the action you choose (such as **Navigation controls** in the example shown). These settings will be taught with the corresponding action.

Conditions are covered in chapter 11.

Edit an Action Trigger

You can edit all aspects of a trigger in the **Trigger Wizard**. You can edit blue hyperlinked attributes of a trigger in the **Triggers** panel.

To edit a trigger in the Trigger Wizard:
1. Select the trigger.
2. Click the **Edit trigger** button.
3. Make your changes in the wizard.
4. Click the **OK** button.

To edit a trigger attribute in the Triggers panel:
1. Click a blue hyperlinked attribute.
2. Select a new value from the drop-down list.

BRIGHT IDEA

When you add a button to your slide, an unconfigured action is added to the **Triggers** panel. Click the **Add trigger** hyperlink to bring up the **Trigger Wizard** for the button.

> **Object Triggers**
> ☐ **Button 1**
> Add trigger

Manage Action Triggers

Copy, Paste, and Delete
To copy and paste or delete selected triggers, use the buttons at the bottom of the **Triggers** panel or keyboard shortcuts:

- Copy = **Ctrl + C**
- Paste = **Ctrl + V**
- Delete = **Delete**

Trigger Order
If you have an object with multiple triggers, the order of the triggers may be important. For example, if you have a game with a score, you'll want to make sure you add or subtract the student's points before running any actions based on those points. Triggers fire from top to bottom. You can rearrange them by using the **Move up** and **Move Down** arrows.

Interactive Objects

You can make just about any object interactive. However, certain objects are specifically designed to be interactive:

- **Hyperlinks**: Hyperlinks let you create a text link with one or more actions.

- **Buttons**: Buttons come with interactive states already set up (such as hover, down, visited, etc.) and one trigger already attached.

- **Check Boxes** and **Radio Buttons**: Use these for custom form elements or questions.

- **Hotspots**: Hotspots are interactive shapes that the student can't see in the published course, but that you can see in the authoring environment. They have one trigger attached already and are usually placed over part of an image that you want the student to click.

- **Markers**: Students click or rollover an icon to view a pop-up window with text and/or media.

- **Data Entry** boxes: This is a text entry box that the student can type into. You can save the information to be used later in the course. You'll learn about data entry boxes in chapter 11.

- **Questions**: You'll learn more about questions in chapter 12.

Add a Hyperlink to Text

Hyperlinks have a default configuration to go to a webpage or launch a document when the user clicks the text.

To add a hyperlink leading to a webpage:

1. Select the text you want to hyperlink.
2. Go to the **Insert** tab.
3. Click the **Hyperlink** button.
4. In the **File** field, enter the web address you want.
5. Click the **Browser options** button to configure the properties of the browser window.
6. Click the **OK** button.

Browser Options, p. 127

To add a hyperlink that launches a document:

1. Select the text you want to hyperlink.
2. Go to the **Insert** tab.
3. Click the **Hyperlink** button.
4. Click the **Load file** button.
5. Find and select the document you want to launch.
6. Click the **Open** button.
7. Click the **OK** button.

POWER TIPS

Even though the **Trigger Wizard** is configured to launch a webpage or document, you can still change any of the fields if you want to set up a different action.

You can apply more than one action to the hyperlink in the **Triggers** panel.

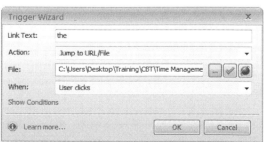

Create a Button

To create a button:

1. Go to the **Insert** menu.
2. Click the **Button** drop-down menu.
3. Select one of the two button options.
4. Click and drag your mouse on the slide to draw the button.
5. Type the text for your button, if needed.

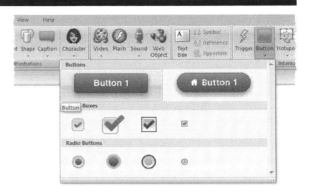

Button Actions

Unlike a hyperlink, the **Trigger Wizard** does not automatically appear when you add a button. There is one trigger already attached, which can be configured in the **Triggers** panel. You can also add additional triggers there.

 Add a Trigger, p. 114

Button States

Buttons automatically come with 6 states:

- Normal: the object as originally created
- Hover: what shows when the student hovers over it
- Down: what shows while the student clicks it
- Visited: what shows after it has been clicked once
- Disabled: what shows when the button is inactive
- Hidden: nothing is shown (This option does not appear with the other options since it cannot be edited.)

You can change the appearance of these states and add or delete states like you can with any other object.

 States, ch. 9

Button Formatting Options

You can format buttons the same way as other shapes, such as changing the size, color, outline, glow, etc.

 Object Properties, ch. 6
Arranging Objects, ch. 7

Icon Buttons

Rather than creating a text button, you can also pull from a library of icons for your buttons.

To add an icon to a button:

1. Go go the **Button Tools: Format** tab.
2. Click the **Button Icons** gallery drop-down arrow. **(A)**
3. Select the icon you want.
4. Use the drop-down menus next to the gallery to change the alignment and color of the icon.

Add Check Boxes and Radio Buttons

Check boxes and radio buttons are individual interactive elements that you can use to create custom form or question functions.

To add a check box or radio button:

1. Go to the **Insert** tab.
2. Click the **Button** drop-down menu.
3. Select the check box or radio button you want.
4. Click on the slide to place the object.

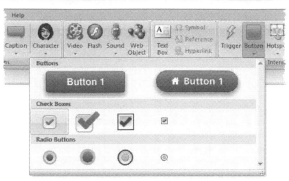

Actions

Check boxes and radio buttons do not come with any actions attached, and they often don't need any. More often than not, you'll use the state of these objects as a condition for an action somewhere else. For example, you might have a **Check My Answer** button that shows one layer or another based on which check box is in the **Selected** state. If you do want to add actions, you can do so in the **Triggers** panel.

 Add a Trigger, p. 114
Conditions, p. 138

States

Check boxes and radio buttons come with similar states as buttons, with one exception. Instead of a **Visited** state, they have a **Selected** state, which, as the name implies, means the object is selected.

 States, ch. 9

Formatting Options

Check boxes and radio buttons have many of the same formatting options as other objects. One major difference is that you can format the box/circle as well as the checkmark/dot.

 Object Properties, ch. 6
Arranging Objects, ch. 7

Labels

To add a text label to the check box or radio button, just select the object, and start typing.

 DESIGN TIPS

- Check boxes are square and let the student select more than one. Radio buttons are round, and only one can be selected at a time.

- Many question slides use check boxes and radio buttons. Depending upon what you are doing, it may be quicker to use a quiz slide, or it may be quicker to add the individual elements yourself.

 BRIGHT IDEA

Be sure to indicate whether you want the initial state to be **Normal** (not selected) or **Selected**. You can do this from the **States** tab or by selecting it on the slide.

Create a Button Set

When you have more than one radio button, the student can only select one. If the student then selects another one, the first one is automatically deselected. But what if you want to have two sets of radio buttons on a page as shown? The student would need to select one radio button in each set, not just one radio button out of all five. You can do that by assigning the radio buttons to different button sets. Only one item can be selected at a time in each button set, and each button set works independently from other button sets.

To add object(s) to an existing button set:
1. Select the objects.
2. Right-click them.
3. Select **Button Set**.
4. Select the button set you want.

To add object(s) to a new button set:
1. Select the objects you want in the new set.
2. Right-click them.
3. Select **Button Set**.
4. Select **New set**.
5. Enter a name for the new set.
6. Click the **Add** button.

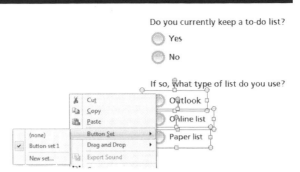

 POWER TIP

Button sets aren't just for radio buttons! You can create a button set for three characters or three buttons, for example. When one is selected, the others are deselected.

Add a Hotspot

Hotspots are interactive shapes that the student cannot see in the published course, but that you can see in edit mode. You can make oval, rectangle, and freeform shapes.

To add a hotspot:
1. Go to the **Insert** tab.
2. Click the **Hotspot** drop-down menu.
3. Select the shape type you want.
4. Click and drag your mouse to draw the shape on the slide.

 Drawing shapes, p. 52

As with buttons, you can format hotspots using standard formatting options and assign the action in the **Triggers** panel.

 DESIGN TIP

Which do you use: hotspot, button, or graphic with a trigger attached? In many cases, all three options would work just fine, and it comes down to a matter of personal preference. Here are a few factors to consider:

- Buttons already have interaction-related states attached (hover, visited, etc.), which might save you time.

- Shapes with triggers manually attached may take longer to set up, but they give you more design flexibility, letting you use any shape, graphic, etc.

- Hotspots are invisible to the student, so they are useful when you want only part of an image to have a certain action, such as parts of a diagram.

Markers

Markers are pre-built interactions consisting of a button **(A)** and a pop-up label **(B)**. By default, when the student rolls his or her mouse over the marker, the title of the text appears. When the student clicks the marker, the full label appears.

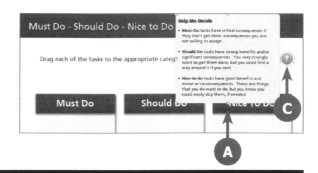

Add a Marker

To add a marker:

1. Go to the **Insert** tab.
2. Click the **Marker** button.
3. Select the marker type you want.
4. Click on the slide where you want the marker to appear.
5. Click in the title placeholder, and type the title.
6. Click in the description placeholder, and type the text for the pop-up.

Label Size and Position

The label can be resized and moved to different sides of the marker. If all the text does not fit, a scrollbar appears.

To resize the label, click and drag the resize handles.

To change the position of the label, click and drag the edge to the position you want. There are 12 "stops" around the marker where you can position the label.

Click to add title

Click to add description

POWER TIP

You can add other triggers to the marker, just like you can with other objects.

Marker Gallery, p. 238

Marker Options

Use the **Marker Tools: Format** tab for formatting and functional options.

Change Icon: Use this drop-down menu to change the icon on the marker.

Sound: Use this menu to add sound that plays when the student clicks on the marker.

Media: Use this menu to add an image or video to the label. You can have one media file per label and can resize and reposition it by clicking and dragging.

 Media, ch. 8

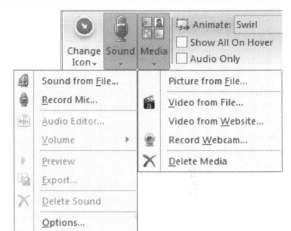

Animate: To help draw the students' attention to the marker, you can have an animation effect. By default, markers have a swirl animation. You can change that to have a pulse animation or no animation.

Show All On Hover: By default, only the title shows when the student hovers over the marker, with the rest of the label appearing on mouse click. Check this box if you'd like the entire label to show up when the student hovers over the marker.

Audio Only: Check this box if you want to have the marker play a sound without showing a label.

Marker Styles: In this section, you have many of the same options for fill and border as you do for other objects. In addition, you can change the color of the marker icon.

Label Styles: In this section, you can format the label fill and border. If you want to apply the same formatting to all labels on the slide, click **Apply to All**. (To change the style of several markers at once, just select them all and make the change.)

Arrange: You can use the same arrangement tools as with other objects.

 Object Properties, ch. 6
Arranging Objects, ch. 7

Action Types

On the following pages, you'll learn some of the specific details of many of the action types.

Change State Action

A change state action (not surprisingly) changes the state of an object on the slide. In addition to selecting the action, trigger, and object, you'll need to select which object will change states (**On Object** field) and which state it should change to (**To state**).

 States, p. 103

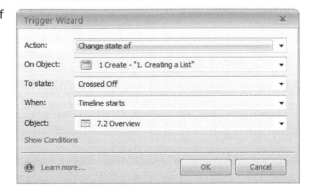

Show Layer/Hide Layer Actions

When you set up a slide layer, it is hidden. Add a **Show layer** action to make a layer visible and a **Hide layer** action if you want to make it hidden again.

If you want to make a layer visible when the slide first loads, add a trigger to the page that starts when the **Timeline** does, as shown.

DESIGN TIP

You can make a layer disappear automatically when it is finished playing. Just add an action to the layer to hide the layer when its **Timeline** ends.

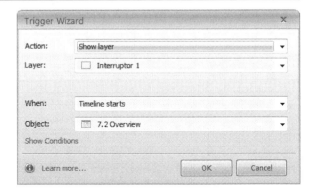

Jump to Slide/Jump to Scene

Use these actions to go to another slide in the story. Use **Jump to slide** to pick a specific slide and **Jump to scene** to go to the first slide in a scene. You can also pick **next slide/next scene** or **previous slide/previous scene**.

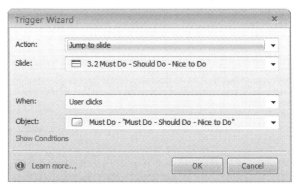

 DESIGN TIP

If you want to go to the beginning of a scene, it is usually better to use **Jump to scene** instead of jumping to the first slide. If you jump to the first slide and then delete or move that slide, your action may not work anymore. But if you jump to the scene, the action always goes to the first slide, even if you rearrange them.

Lightbox Slide/Close Lightbox Actions

A lightbox is a slide that appears as a pop-up window on top of the current slide, with the current slide grayed out and disabled.

When you use the **Lightbox slide** action, you indicate which slide you want to have appear and whether or not you want the navigational controls (**Prev**, **Next**, **Submit**) on the lightboxed slide.

Lightboxed slides come with a red **X** as a close button. However, you can create a **Close Lightbox** trigger. For example, you might want to make your own close button that is more prominent or have the lightbox close automatically when the slide is done playing.

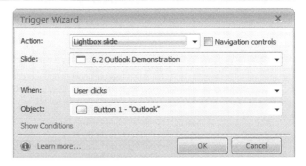

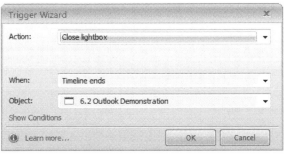

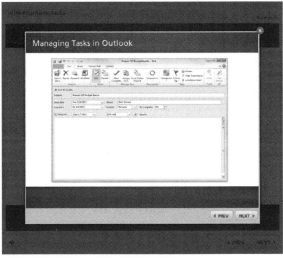

Lightbox slide with navigation controls

 ## CAUTION

- If you decide to show navigation controls, make sure the lightboxed slides have the controls enabled in **Slide Properties**.

- A lightboxed slide appears slightly smaller than its full slide. Consider this reduction in size when deciding on font and image sizes for a slide that will become a lightbox.

 ## DESIGN TIP

Navigation controls are useful when you want to show several slides in the pop-up window. For example, you might show a short tutorial on how to use the course. Put all the tutorial slides in one scene, and then lightbox the first slide with navigational controls enabled. Then the student can click through all the slides.

Play/Pause/Stop Media Actions

The play, pause, and stop actions let you control audio and video on your slides independently of the **Timeline**. For example, if you pause the audio narration on the slide with one of these actions, the **Timeline** keeps playing and any other objects continue to appear/disappear accordingly. If you have more than one media object on the slide, a media action only affects the media object selected in the **Trigger Wizard**, not the other media on the slide.

Play Media

If you add audio or video using the **Insert Sound** or **Insert Video** function on the **Insert** tab, the media automatically starts playing when the **Timeline** does—you don't need an action for that. You would need the **Play media** action if:

- You want to add media that does not play automatically when the **Timeline** starts. If you add the media from the **Play media Trigger Wizard** (instead of the **Insert** menu) that media does NOT automatically play. It does not play until the **Play Media** action is triggered.

- You are using the **Pause media** or **Stop media** actions. If you pause or stop the media for any reason (such as giving the student stop and pause control), then you'll probably want a play control to let them start again.

When setting up the **Play** media action, you'll select what media you want to control from the **Media** drop-down menu. You can select a media file already on the slide or choose to import or record sound or video.

Stop Media and Pause Media

What's the difference between **Stop media** and **Pause media**? When you stop the media, it returns to its starting point. If you play the media from there, it picks up at the beginning. If you pause the media, it remains where it was paused, picking up again there if you play the media.

Media: unassigned

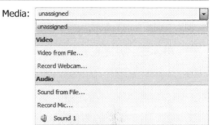

 Media, ch. 8

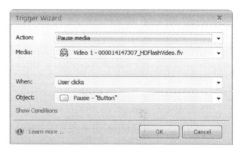

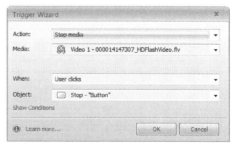

POWER TIP

You can combine the media actions with variables to create user preferences. For example, you can have a question at the beginning of the course asking students if they want to listen to the audio. Then on each slide, include an action that stops the audio if the student answered yes to that question.

 Conditions, p. 138
Variables, p. 133

DESIGN TIP

Remember that the button icons include symbols for working with media.

 Button icons, p. 117

Restart Course/Exit Course

The **Restart Course** action returns the student to the starting scene and resets all variables, states, etc.

The **Exit Course** button closes the course window.

Jump to URL/File

Use this action to either link to a webpage or launch a document.

To link to a webpage:

1. In the **File** field, enter the web address you want.
2. Click the **Browser options** button to configure the properties of the browser window.
3. Click the **OK** button.

To launch a document:

1. Click the **Load file** button.
2. Find and select the document you want to launch.
3. Click the **Open** button.
4. Click the **OK** button.

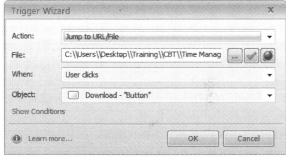

Browser Options

Window

Indicate if you want the webpage to display in the current browser window (replacing the course) or open up a new browser window to display the webpage.

Browser Controls

Use this field to determine what controls display in the student's browser.

- **Default**: Use whatever settings the student has for new browser windows.
- **No address bar**: Leave all controls except the address bar. This is useful when the students are using computers on which access to websites is restricted.
- **No browser controls**: Remove all controls from the browser, including the address bar, back button, favorites, etc. Removing all controls can help keep the student focused on the page you are sending them to.

Window Size

- **Default**: Use whatever size the student's browser determines.
- **Full-screen**: Open the student's browser window full screen.
- **Custom**: Enter your own width and height for the browser window. Using a smaller browser window is useful if you want the student to see the webpage and the course at the same time.

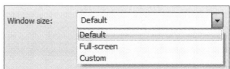

Send Email to

The **Send Email** to action opens the student's default email program, addressed to the address in the **Email** field. You can enter more than one email address separated by semicolons.

 CAUTION

Students must have an email program installed on their computer (such as Outlook) for this action to work. It will not work with a web-based email system (such as Gmail).

Execute JavaScript

The **Execute JavaScript** action lets you include custom JavaScript to add functionality that does not come automatically with Storyline.

For example:

- If you are creating a game, you might want some custom functionality that Storyline doesn't offer.
- You want to include the date or time in the course.
- You want to customize how the course interacts with a Learning Management System.

To add JavaScript, click the **Browse** button **(A)**, and type or paste your code in the pop-up wiindow.

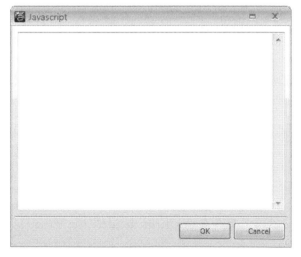

Drag-and-Drop Interactions

To create a drag-and-drop interaction, you don't need to add interactive objects, such as buttons or checkboxes. Instead, you use regular objects, such as shapes and text boxes, and action triggers based on dragging events or dropping events. This lets you designate an object as "draggable" that can trigger certain actions (such as displaying a layer with feedback) when that object is dropped on something.

 BRIGHT IDEA

You can also set up a drag-and-drop question using the **Freeform** question type.

 Freeform Questions, p. 157

Object Dragged Over Event

Use this event when you want to have something happen when the student drags an object over another, without necessarily dropping it. For example, you might want to have an object glow (change state) when an object is over it so that the student knows that it is a potential drop target.

When you use this event, you will need to select which object can be dragged, and which objects(s) fire the action when dragged over.

Object Dropped On Event

Use this event when you want to have something happen when a student drops a dragged item on top of another object. For example, you might want to display a layer with correct feedback if it is dropped on one item, and a layer with incorrect feedback if it is dropped a different object.

When you use this event, you will need to select which object can be dragged and which object(s) fire the action when dropped on.

Notes

Advanced Actions & Variables

11

Introduction

In this chapter, you'll learn about more building blocks to help you create custom interactions and functionality. Specifically, you'll learn how to save and store bits of information, called variables, and then display the information to the student or use it to set up conditional logic.

For example, you might:

- Build a game that keeps score (stored in a variable) with a scoreboard shown to the students.
- Ask the students to enter their names (stored in a variable), and then customize messages with the students' names.
- Ask the students whether they are managers or non-managers (stored in a variable), and then show certain information based on their answers (conditional logic based on the variable).

In This Chapter

- About Variables
- Creating Variables
- Modifying Variables
- Managing Variables
- Displaying Variables
- Data Entry Boxes
- Conditional Logic

Notes

Working With Variables

Variables are pieces of information stored within the course that can be displayed to the student or used to set up conditional, if/then logic. You can either add variables yourself (such as to keep track of points in a game you make) or add interactive objects (such as text entry boxes) that come with a variable already attached. The value of that variable can then be adjusted by you with an action trigger (such as adding points to the score) or by the student (such as by clicking a button to indicate a preference).

1. Create	2. Adjust	3. Use

1. Create the variable	2. Adjust the variable	3. Use the variable
Add a text entry box (which has a variable attached).	The student enters his or her name.	Show the student's name on a certificate.
Add a variable called "points."	Set up an action that adds one point if the student answers a question correctly.	Put a scoreboard on the screen that shows the student's score.
Add a variable called "manager."	The student clicks one of two buttons which changes the variable to "yes" or "no."	Create a conditional action that goes to page 3 if the variable is "yes" or page 4 if it is "no."

Create a Variable

To manually create a variable:

1. In the **Triggers** panel, click the **Manage Project Variables** button. **(A)**
2. Click the **Create a new variable** button. **(B)**
3. In the **Name** field, type a name for your variable.
4. In the **Type** field, select the type of data the variable will contain.
5. In the **Value** field, enter the starting value for the variable (optional).
6. Click the **OK** button.
7. Click the **OK** button again.

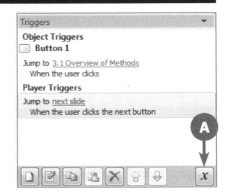

 BRIGHT IDEAS

- No two variables can have the same name, so be sure to use a unique name each time.

- Variables can contain letters and numbers only—no spaces or special characters.

- When selecting the type, your options are **Text**, **Number**, or **True/False** (similar to yes/no).

- If you add a data entry box or a results slide, related variables are automatically created for you. **(C)**

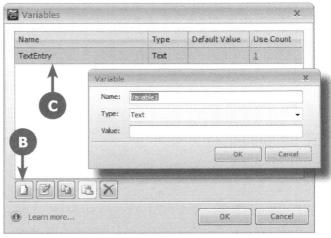

Adjust Variable Action

To change the value of a variable (or have the student do so), you just need to add a trigger with the **Adjust Variable** action.

To add an Adjust Variable action:

1. Select the object you want to add the trigger to (optional).
2. Click the **Add New Trigger** button.
3. In the **Action** drop-down menu, select **Adjust Variable**.
4. In the **Variable** menu, select the variable you want to adjust.
5. In the **Operator** field, indicate the type of assignment you want to make (see below).
6. In the first **Value** field, select **Value** or **Variable** (see below).
7. In the second **Value** field, enter what you want to change the variable to.
8. In the **When** drop-down menu, select the event that will trigger the action.
9. In the **Object** menu, select the item to be used as the trigger.
10. Click the **OK** button.

Operator

Your choices for the operator vary based on the data type of the variable.

- **Assignment**: Available for all data types, use this action to change the current value to what you enter in the **Value** field.

- **Not Assignment**: For true/false variable types, use this to toggle the variable to the opposite value. **True** becomes **False**, and **False** becomes **True**.

- **Mathematical**: If you are working with a number, you can add, subtract, multiply, or divide.

Value

The **Value** drop-down menu has two choices:

- **Value**: Use **Value** when you want to enter a fixed new value in the field provided, such as a number or text. If you are working with a true/false variable, you can select either **True** or **False**.

- **Variable**: Use **Variable** when you want to modify the variable using the value of another variable. For example, you may want to add the points from a question (stored in a variable) to the variable storing the overall score.

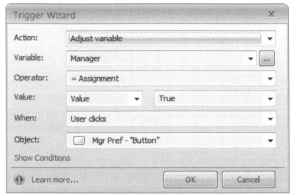

Change the variable "Manager" to be "True" when the student clicks a button.

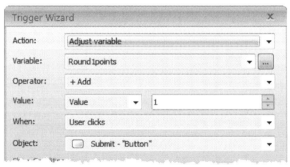

Add 1 point to the variable "Round1points" when the user clicks a button.

Add the points from "Round1points" to the variable "TotalPoints."

 TIME SAVER

If you haven't already created the variable you want to adjust, click the **Browse** button in the **Variable** field to add it right there.

Manage Variables

Variables do not belong to a specific slide, but rather belong to the project as a whole. You can manage the variables from **Story View** or any slide by clicking the **Manage Course Variables** button in the **Triggers** panel. **(A)**

To edit a variable:
1. Select the variable you want to edit.
2. Click the **Edit the selected variable** button.
3. Make your changes.
4. Click the **OK** button.

To copy and paste a variable:
1. Select the variable you want to copy.
2. Click the **Copy the selected variable** button.
3. Click the **Paste the copied variable...** button.

To delete a variable:
1. Select the variable you want to delete.
2. Click the **Delete the selected variable** button.

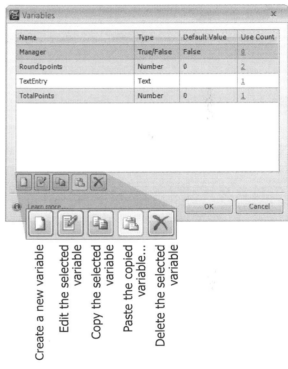

Display a Variable Value

You can display the value of a variable to the student in an object that contains text (text box, button, etc.). The value updates dynamically anytime the underlying variable changes. In edit mode, you'll see the name of the variable. But in preview mode or the published course, you'll see the value of the variable.

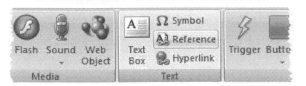

To display a variable value:

1. Place your cursor in the text where you want the value to appear.
2. Go to the **Insert** tab.
3. Select **Reference**.
4. Select the variable whose value you want to include.
5. Click the **OK** button.

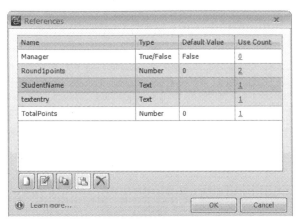

 CAUTION

Objects that have a variable reference will autofit the text from the variable. If the variable has a lot of text, the font size may get very small. Be sure to test what this looks like, especially if the student is entering the value.

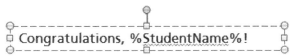

Variable reference in edit mode

Congratulations, Jeremy Williams!

Variable reference in preview mode

Data Entry Boxes

A data entry box lets the student type a response of some sort. You can have a data entry box that accepts alphanumeric characters or a numeric entry box that only accepts numbers.

You might want to use a data entry box to have the student:

- Enter his or her name.
- Answer a question.
- Write down thoughts for a "think about it" question.

The student's response is saved in the course as a variable. You can then use that response to:

- Display the entry back to the student later.
- Perform an action (such as showing a layer, changing a state, or going to another slide) based on what the student entered.
- Perform calculations, such as adding up a total.
- Simply stay on the page for the student to consider and possibly print.

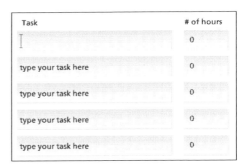

Add a Data Entry Box

To add a data entry box:

1. Go to the **Insert** tab.
2. Click the **Data Entry** drop-down button.
3. Select **Text Entry** or **Numeric Entry**.
4. Click and drag your mouse on the slide to draw the box.

Options

Appearance

- Once your data entry box is on the slide, you can format it like any other object.
- Text entry boxes have default text that can serve as instructions for the student. If you want to change the text, simply type new text in the box.

Variables

- When you add a data entry box, a trigger is automatically added to the slide **(A)** that creates a new variable and stores the student's answer in it. You can then use the answer like you can any other variable.
- If you'd like to change the name of the variable (from **TextEntry1** to **Task1**, for example), click the **Manage Project Variables** button **(B),** and change the name in the **Variables** dialog box. **(C)**
- If you'd like to send the value to a different variable than the one created automatically, select the trigger in the **Triggers** panel, and then click the **Edit Selected Triggers** button. **(D)** In the **Trigger Wizard** dialog box, either select an existing variable, or click the **New variable** button **(E)** to create a new one.

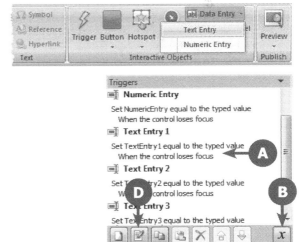

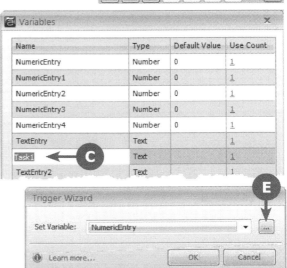

Conditional Logic

Conditions let you create action triggers that only "fire" if certain conditions are met, for example, if all the buttons on the page have been visited, or if the student selects option B on a question.

There are three factors you can use for conditions:

- **Variables**: You can set conditions based on whether a variable value does or does not meet certain criteria.

- **Shapes**: You can set conditions based on an object's state.

- **Window**: You can set conditions based on whether the page being evaluated is a regular course page or a lightboxed page.

Based on the factor being considered and the type of variable, you can choose one of the following methods of evaluation (operators):

- **Equal to**: The condition is met if the item being evaluated is the same as what's in the **Value** field. On text fields, you can indicate whether or not you want to ignore the case (capitalization).

- **Not equal to**: The condition is met if the item being evaluated is anything other than what's in the **Value** field. Again, you can indicate whether or not to ignore case on text fields.

- **Numerical operators**: If you are working with a numerical variable, you have the additional options of **Less than**, **Greater than**, **Less than or equal to**, **Greater than or equal to**, or **Between two values**.

- **Window operators**: If the element being considered is a window, you have two choices: **this slide is lightboxed** or **this slide is inside the player frame**.

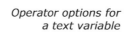
Action trigger with a condition

Condition set-up dialog box

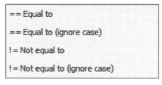
Operator options for a text variable

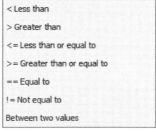
Operator options for a numerical variable

Operator options for a window

Add a Condition to an Action

To add a condition based on a variable (C):

1. Click the **Show Conditions** link in the **Trigger Wizard** for that action. **(A)**
2. Click the **Add** button. **(B)**
3. In the **List** field, select **Variables**.
4. In the **If** field, select the variable you want to evaluate.
5. In the **Operator** field, select the type of logic you want to use for evaluation.
6. In the **Type** field, select **Value** to compare against a value you enter or **Variable** to compare against an existing variable's value.
7. In the **Value** field, enter the specific value to be evaluated against.

To add a condition based on the state of an object (D):

1. Click the **Show Conditions** link in the **Trigger Wizard** for that action.
2. Click the **Add** button.
3. In the **List** field, select **Shapes**.
4. In the **If** field, select the object you want to evaluate.
5. In the **Operator** field, select **Equal to** or **Not equal to.**
6. In the **State** field, select the state to be evaluated against.

To add a condition based on a window (E):

1. Click the **Show Conditions** link in the **Trigger Wizard** for that action.
2. Click the **Add** button.
3. In the **List** field, select **Window**.
4. In the **If** field, select **this slide is lightboxed** or **this slide is inside the player frame**.

POWER TIP

You can have more than one condition on an action. When you do, indicate if you want all of the conditions to be met for the action to fire (select **AND**) or if you only need one of the conditions to be met (select **OR**). **(F)**

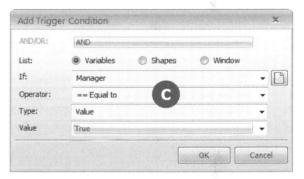

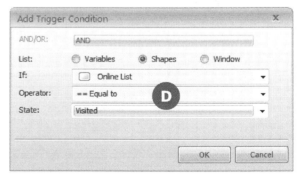

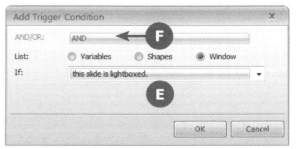

Manage Conditions

To edit a condition:
1. Select the condition you want to edit.
2. Click the **Edit selected condition** button.
3. Make the changes you want.
4. Click the **OK** button.

To delete a condition:
1. Select the condition you want to edit.
2. Click the **Delete the selected condition** button.

 TIME SAVER

Certain aspects of a condition can be edited right from the **Triggers** panel. Just select a blue hyperlinked element, and select a new option from the drop-down menu that appears.

Questions & Quizzes

Introduction

In addition to the interactive elements you learned how to use in chapters 10 and 11, Storyline also comes with a question editor, making it easy to set up questions, feedback, scoring, and branching.

In this chapter, you'll learn how to add and configure questions using the question editor, plus how to combine them into a formal, scored quiz using results slides.

In This Chapter

- Adding Questions
- Question Types
- Adding Content
- Editing Questions
- Question Options
- Feedback, Scoring, and Branching
- Question Banks
- Results Slides
- Quiz-Related Variables and Actions

Notes

Adding Questions

Questions are as easy to insert as any other slide. Once you add a question slide, you can then add the question content, feedback, and logic in the question editor. However, you aren't limited to using the question editor. You can also work with your questions in **Slide** view, letting you bring in many of the elements you might use on any other slide, such as videos, graphics, action triggers, etc.

Insert a Question

To insert a question:

1. Go to the **Home** tab in **Story View** or **Slide** view.
2. Click the **New Slide** button.
3. Click the **Quizzing** tab down the left side of the dialog box.
4. Select the question category from the tabs across the top of the dialog box.
5. Select the question format you want.
6. Click the **Insert** button.

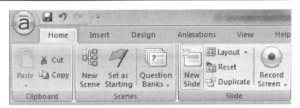

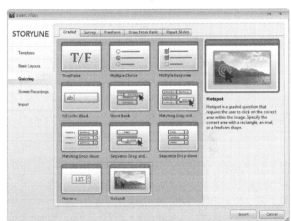

Graded Question Gallery

Question Type	Example
True/False Student decides between two options, labeled "True" and "False" by default. • Change the labels to suit the question: yes/no, allowed/not allowed, etc. • Provide question- or answer-level scoring and feedback.	Decide if the following statement is true or false. Tasks are easier to prioritize if they are written down or typed. ◉ True ◯ False
Multiple Choice **Standard**: Student decides between multiple options, with only one correct answer. **Word Bank**: Student chooses the correct answer from a list and drags it up to the placeholder at the top. • Enter up to 10 answer choices. • Provide question- or answer-level scoring and feedback.	Which to-do list method is the best? ◯ Paper list ◯ Outlook list ◯ Online list ◉ It depends. When your boss comes in your office with a new request, you should: evaluate it in relation to your other priorities politely tell her you don't have time. put it at the top of your list. put it at the bottom of your list
Multiple Response Student decides between multiple options, with more than one correct answer. • Enter up to 10 answer choices. • Provide feedback and scoring at the question level only.	Which of the following statements apply to a Must-Do task? Select all that apply. ☑ Significant benefits for doing it ☑ Serious consequences for not doing it ☐ Flexible deadline
Fill in the Blank Student types an answer in the blank. • Choose whether answer is case sensitive. • Allow for more than one possible answer. • Provide feedback and scoring at the question level only.	Analyzing only two tasks at a time is called a _____ comparison. paired
Numeric Student types a number in the blank. • Grade answers based on a single number, a range of numbers, or both. • Provide feedback and scoring at the question level only.	What is the maximum percentage of tasks that can be on your Must Do list? 40

Graded Question Gallery (cont'd)

Question Type	Example
Matching **Drag and Drop:** Student selects an item on the right and drags it to its match on the left. **Drop-Down**: Student matches items on the left with items in a drop-down menu on the right. • Include up to 10 matches. • Score question based on all matches being correct. • Provide feedback and scoring at the question level only.	Determine which tasks fall into which prioritization category. Submit government audit paperwork due Friday Revise archiving system — Nice to do Prepare for Thursday's staff meeting — Must do Determine which tasks fall into which prioritization category. Submit government audit paperwork by Friday — --Select-- Revise archiving system — --Select-- Prepare for Thursday's staff meeting — --Select-- Should do Nice to do Must do
Sequence Drag and Drop **Drag and Drop:** Students drag and drop items into the correct sequence. **Drop-Down**: Students place items in sequence by selecting them from drop-down lists. • Include up to 10 items. • Score answers based on the entire sequence being correct. • Provide feedback and scoring at the question level only.	Put the steps for postponing a task in the proper order. 1. Reschedule 2. Decline 3. Acknowledge Reschedule Put the steps for postponing a task into the proper order. Acknowledge Decline --Select-- Reschedule Decline Acknowledge
Hotspot Student clicks on a specific point in a graphic. • Designate correct response using drawing tools. • Provide feedback at the question level only.	Based on this paired comparison, click on the task you should do first. Review vendor bids ✓✓ Revise archiving system Prepare for staff meeting ✓✓✓ Submit audit paperwork ✓✓✓✓ Write performance evaluations ✓

Survey Question Gallery

Question Type	Example
Likert Scale Students rate statements on a scale, such as 1-5 or strongly agree to strongly disagree. • Enter up to 10 statements to be evaluated. • Create your own scale with up to 10 options. • Provide one feedback message.	Evaluate the following statements and rate how often you do them. 1 2 3 4 5 Each week I make a list of what I hope to accomplish that week. ● ○ ○ ○ ○ (Sometimes) Each morning I review the list and decide what to work on that day. ○ ○ ● ○ ○ When I receive a new request, I evaluate how important it is in comparison to what was already on my list. ○ ○ ○ ○ ○ I have realistic expectations about what I can accomplish in a day, a week. ○ ○ ○ ○ ○ If I have more on my list to do than I'll have time to do, I talk to my boss about priorities. ○ ○ ○ ○ ○
Short Answer Student types an answer to an open-ended question. • Use for responses up to 256 characters. • Use for "reflection" questions or self-graded questions. • Provide one feedback message.	What two things are you going to do differently as a result of taking this course? Make a list every week and make sure that I look at it every morning.
Essay Student types an answer to an open-ended question. • Can limit the number of characters or leave unlimited. • Use for "reflection" questions or self-graded questions. • Provide one feedback message.	What are some concerns you might have about saying "no" to your boss? I won't be seen as a team player. He will make me do it anyway. It will look like I can't manage my time. There's no one else to give the work to. It may affect raises, assignments, and promotions.
Other Survey Question Types In addition to the survey question types shown above, there are six other survey question types that mimic graded questions. The only difference is that they are not graded and offer only one feedback option. • Pick One = Multiple Choice • Pick Many = Multiple Response • Which Word = Word Bank • Ranking Drag and Drop = Sequence Drag and Drop • Ranking Drop-Down = Sequence Drag and Drop • How Many = Numeric	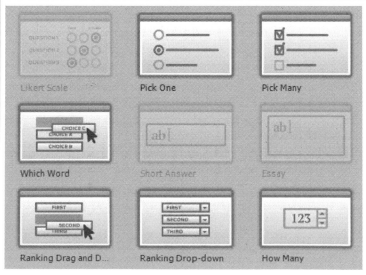

Freeform Question Gallery

	Example
Drag and Drop Students drag objects such as text boxes, images, or shapes onto drop targets. • Set up multiple drop items to go into the same drop target. • Have drop items that don't belong in any drop areas or vice versa.	
Pick One Student decides between multiple options, with only one correct answer. • Use shapes, images, etc. as the choices instead of radio buttons with text.	
Pick Many Student decides between multiple options, with more than one answer correct. • Use shapes, images, etc. as the choices, instead of check boxes with text.	
Shortcut Keys Student types a shortcut key or keystroke combination.	Type the keyboard shortcut for adding a new task in Outlook.
Text Entry and Hotspot These two options work exactly the same way as the **Text Entry** and **Hotspot** questions available from the **Insert Slides** dialog box. Use the freeform version if you already have a slide that you want to change to a question rather than create a new slide.	

Adding Question Content

When you insert a new question slide, the slide is inserted with the question, and the question editor automatically opens. Here you can add your question content in the form, add feedback, and configure question logic. This next section covers how to add question content in the editor for each of the question types. Later in the chapter, you'll learn how to edit the question in **Slide** view, add feedback, and set up the logic, which is mostly the same for all question types.

When you finish adding your content and configuring the settings, click the **Save & Close** button to return to **Slide** view, where you can make changes to the layout and formatting. (See page 163.)

True/False

Enter the Question

Type your instructions and the statement to be evaluated in this field.

Enter the Choices

- Click the radio button for the correct option.
- Double-click in the **Choice** fields to edit the text labels if you want something other than "True" and "False."

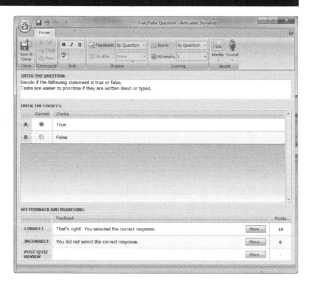

 DESIGN TIPS

Avoid these common traps with true/false questions:

- Even though this is a question, students are evaluating a statement. So be sure the statement ends with a period and not a question mark.
- Avoid statements with the words "never," "only," or "always." These are clues to the savvy test-taker that the answer is "False."
- Avoid negative statements. It can be confusing to know whether to choose "True" or "False" when the statement is NOT something. Or, the student may not see the word "not." If you do decide to use a negative, emphasize "not" with bolding, etc.

Multiple Choice, Word Bank, and Multiple Response

Even though multiple-choice and word bank questions look very different on-screen, the form behind them is identical. Multiple-response forms are the same with one variation—the ability to mark more than one as correct.

Enter the Question

Enter your question and instructions.

Enter the Choices

- In each line, enter one of the possible answers.

- For multiple-choice and word bank questions, select the radio button for the correct answer. For multiple response, check the check box for all of the correct answers.

- Click and drag choices up and down if you need to rearrange them.

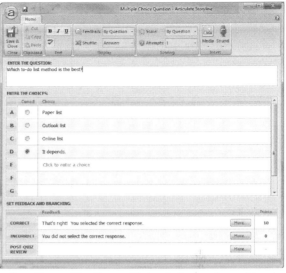

Question editor for multiple choice and word bank

Question editor for multiple response

DESIGN TIPS

Avoid these common traps with multiple-choice questions:

- If you are going to shuffle the choices in the published course, be sure not to use "All of the above" or "None of the above," as they could be shuffled to the top of the list. Instead, use "All of these" or "None of these."

- It is common for test creators to use "All of these" and "None of these" only when they are the correct answer, making it a clue to the savvy test-taker that it is the right answer. When using these choices, be sure to include them as the wrong answer in a few questions.

- Be sure to include clear instructions. Students need to know that they can select more than one response in a multiple-response question or that they are supposed to drag the answer to the placeholder in a word bank question.

Fill in the Blank

Enter the Question:

Enter your statement and instructions. Use the underscore key to create the blank.

Enter Acceptable Answers

Enter one or more acceptable answers. The question is graded as correct if the student types any one of the acceptable answers.

Options

By default, the student's answer is graded when he or she clicks the **Submit** button in the player controls. You can also use any of the following options:

- **Submit Keys**: Click in the field, and then, using your keyboard, type the key you want to use. Click the **X** button to clear the submit key you entered.

- **Submit Button**: Select from objects currently on the slide, a new hotspot, or a new button.

Answers are case sensitive: Check this box if the student has to match your capitalization. Leave it unchecked if capitalization doesn't matter.

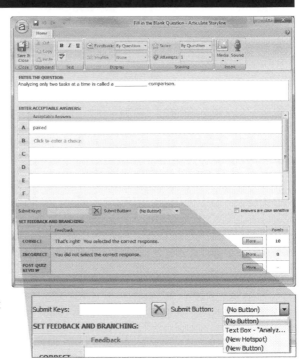

DESIGN TIPS

Avoid these common traps with fill-in-the-blank questions:

- Avoid using fill-in-the-blank questions when you have a subjective question. Just because you know what answer you are looking for, that doesn't mean the students will.

- Answers that could be phrased many different ways can be difficult to grade accurately. If you find yourself entering lots of alternatives, you may be better off using a multiple-choice question instead.

Matching

Whether you use the matching drag and drop or the matching drop-down format, the set-up form is exactly the same.

Enter the Question

Enter your instructions.

Enter the Choices

- On each line, enter a correct matching pair. When the question is published, the items on the left stay in the order as the form, and the items on the right will be shuffled.

- If you want to rearrange the order of the items on the left, click and drag the entry up or down.

DESIGN TIPS

Avoid these common traps with matching questions:

- The size of the "pieces" in a drag-and-drop matching question is fairly fixed. Long choices can lead to small type that may be difficult to read. You have more flexibility on space with the drop-down matching format.

- Choices cannot be used more than once with these question types.

Sequence

The sequence drag and drop and the sequence drop-down formats work exactly the same in the question editor.

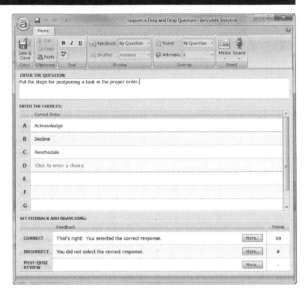

Enter the Question

Enter your instructions here.

Enter the Choices

- Type in each of the steps in the correct order. When the question is published or previewed, the options are shuffled.

- If you need to change the correct order of the steps in the form, click and drag a choice up or down.

Numeric

The numeric question type is much like a fill-in-the-blank question, with two key differences:

- Only numbers are accepted in the entry box.
- Instead of listing the specific numbers that are considered correct, you can set up logic to grade the answer.

Enter the Question

Type your question and instructions here.

Enter the Acceptable Numeric Values

- If you just need to accept a single number as correct, select **Equal to** in the first row and the correct number next to it.
- If you'd like to have more than one specific number as correct, repeat the step above in subsequent rows.
- If there are more correct answers than you want to enter individually, you can use the **Value is** drop-down menu to create a range. For example, you might want to accept any answer under 20.
- If you have more than one acceptable answers, select **Any** or **All** from the drop-down menu under the list of options. **(A) Any** means that only one of the conditions needs to be true. **All** means that all of the conditions must be true.

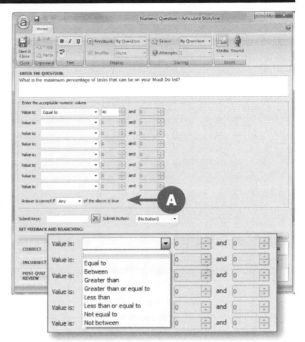

Options

Just as with a fill-in-the-blank question, the question is graded when the student clicks the **Submit** button in the player. You can also set up one of the following options to grade the question:

- **Submit Keys**: Click in the field, and then on your keyboard, type the key you want to use. Click the **X** button to clear the submit key.
- **Submit Button**: Select from objects currently on the slide, a new hotspot, or a new button.

Hotspot

In a hotspot question, the student needs to click on a certain point on the slide, usually part of an image. To set up the question, you'll need to have the image and then indicate which part of it is considered correct.

The incorrect parts of the image can be done in one of two ways. If you only put one hotspot on the slide, then any other point on the slide is considered incorrect. However, you can also put multiple hotspots on the slide. You can then indicate which hotspot is correct and which are incorrect. If the student clicks somewhere other than the correct and incorrect hotspots, nothing happens.

Enter the Question

Type your question and instructions here.

Add Hotspot Areas

- In this section, you see a thumbnail of the slide. You can add your image either by first adding it/creating it on the slide itself, or clicking the **Choose Image** button and importing an image. You cannot modify the image on the slide in this view, but you can go back to the **Slide** view to make any changes you want to the size, layout, etc.

- Next, add one or more hotspots. Click the **Add Hotspot** drop-down menu, and select the type of shape you want to use: oval, rectangle, or freeform. Then, draw the shape on the slide thumbnail.

 Drawing Shapes, p. 52

- Continue to add additional hotspots, if needed.

Edit the Hotspots

- If you only have one hotspot, you don't need to do anything here. However, if you have more than one hotspot, select the radio button for the one that is correct.

- You can also rename the hotspots so that they make more sense to you (as in the sample shown).

- To delete a hotspot, select it either on the thumbnail or in the edit list, and click the **X** button below the thumbnail.

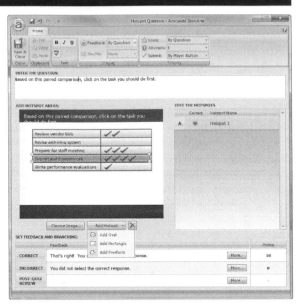

Hotspot question with only a correct hotspot

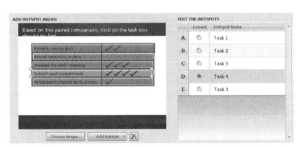

Hotspot question with correct and incorrect hotspots

 DESIGN TIPS

- Why would you want to designate incorrect hotspots? Primarily if you want to set up branching, feedback, or scoring based on WHICH incorrect spot the student clicked. You can only do this if you designate the different possible incorrect answers.

- Remember that with hotspots, the clickable area appears shaded in edit mode, but appears transparent in the published or previewed question. In a hotspot question, the correct hotspot is shaded green and the incorrect hotspots are shaded red.

Survey Questions

Survey questions are set up very much like graded questions, with a few key exceptions:

- There is no classification of right versus wrong.

- You cannot assign points.

- You can have one feedback message, which, if you choose to include it, is displayed regardless of how the student answers the question.

Remember that six of the survey question types are the same as graded question types (see page 146). The other three types are unique to survey questions and are explained here. The images shown here include the feedback option. Please note that feedback is turned off by default on survey questions.

 **DESIGN TIP**

If there are no right or wrong answers, why would you want any feedback? You might want to:

- Thank the students for the response.

- Give the students a "best practice" example to compare their answers to.

- Give them something to think about in relation to their answers.

Likert Scale

In a Likert scale question, students rate one or more statements based on a scale, such as **Agree** to **Disagree**.

Enter the Instructions

Type the instructions for the student here.

Enter the Statements

- In each row, type a statement to be evaluated by the student.

- Click and drag statements if you need to rearrange the order.

Scale

- By default, these questions use a five-point scale of **Strongly Disagree** to **Strongly Agree,** as shown on the right. Click the **Scale** button to change the labels.

- You can include up to 10 points on the scale.

- The scale label is displayed when the mouse hovers over the radio button for that column.

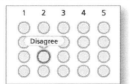

Student's mouse hovered over radio button in the published course

- Uncheck the box at the bottom of the **Likert Scale** dialog box if you don't want the numbers at the top of each column.

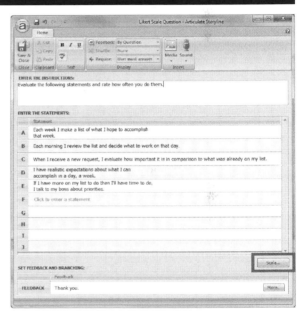

Short Answer and Essay

Both short answer and essay question types let the student type a response. Short answer responses are limited to 256 characters. Essay questions do not have a limit by default, but can be given one. In addition, the text entry box for an essay question uses a scroll bar, meaning you can have a relatively small box on the slide, even if the students' answers will be long.

Enter the Question

Type your question and instructions here.

Maximum Number of Characters

On essay questions, you can limit the number of characters a student can enter.

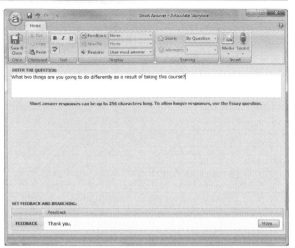

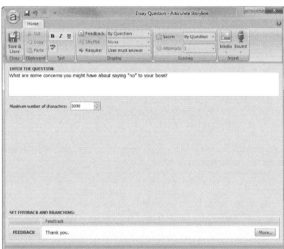

 DESIGN TIPS

Even though the answers to these questions are not graded by the system, you can still have the students evaluate their answers, if appropriate. For example, you can branch to another slide that provides different ways they might have answered the question and why, letting the students compare their answers to yours.

Freeform Questions

Freeform questions let you create a more custom question while still using the underlying logic of the question editor. For example, you can create a multiple-choice question where the student selects a graphic instead of clicking a radio button. You can either insert a new freeform question from the **Insert Slides** dialog box, or you can convert an existing slide to a freeform question.

When you insert a new freeform question from the **Insert Slides** dialog box, it doesn't work exactly as it does for a graded or survey question. With a freeform question, the question editor does not automatically open. Instead, the slide stays in **Slide** view so you can add the elements for the question. When you are ready, you can click the **Edit** button above the **Triggers** panel **(A)** to open the question editor and set up the question logic.

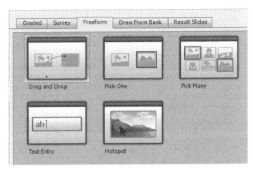

Freeform question types available in the Insert Slides dialog box

Freeform Pick One and Pick Many

Adding Content Objects

Freeform questions start with no content, so you first need to add the objects that the student will select to answer the question. You must add at least two compatible objects to the slide before the **Edit** button appears, letting you open the question editor. Compatible objects include:

- Images
- Hotspots
- Shapes
- Check boxes
- Text boxes
- Radio buttons
- Buttons

You also need to add the question and instructions directly on the slide, rather than through the editor.

Question Editor

Once you have the objects on the slide that the student can select, click the **Edit** button **(A)**. This takes you to the question editor where you can designate right and wrong answers and set up other question logic.

Enter the Choices

- Instead of typing in text for your choices, use the drop-down menu to select the objects from the slide you want to use instead.

- As with a regular question, select the radio button (for pick one) or check boxes (for pick many) for the correct answer(s).

 BRIGHT IDEA

When you designate an object as a question choice, a **Selected** state is added to the object. Go to the **States** tab if you want to change that state's effect.

 States, ch. 9

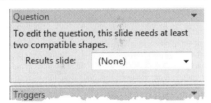

*Question panel **before** having two selectable objects*

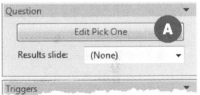

*Question panel **after** having two selectable objects*

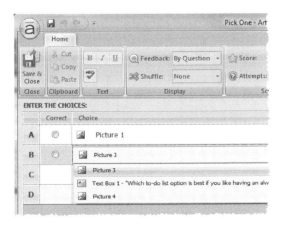

Freeform Drag and Drop Questions

With a drag and drop question, you designate certain objects that students drag and certain objects that the drag items are dropped onto.

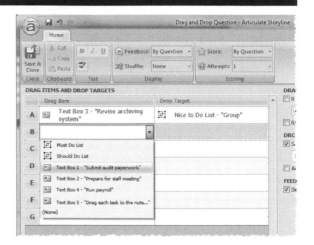

Adding Content Objects

- On the slide, add the items to be dragged and the objects that define the area that the drag items can be dropped onto (targets).

- When you are done, click the **Edit** button (above the **Triggers** panel) to set up the correct drag/drop pairings.

- You will need to add your instructions directly on the slide as well.

Drag Items and Drop Targets

- In the **Drag Item** column, select the first draggable item.

- In the **Drop Target** column, select the correct drop area for that drag item.

- Continue with the same process for the next rows.

- If you have a drag item or a drop target that is not being used (does not have a correct pairing), select it from the list, and then select **None** in the other column to indicate it does not have a match.

Freeform Drag and Drop Questions (cont'd)

Drag Item Options

Return item to start...: By default, the student can drag the item anywhere on the page, and it stays there. Check this box if you want the drop item to return to its start point in one of two situations:

- If the student drops the item anywhere other than on the correct answer (giving them immediate feedback that it isn't the correct answer without telling them what actually is).

- If the student drops the item somewhere that isn't a drop target at all.

Reveal drag items one at a time: Check this box if you don't want to start out showing all of the drag items. When checked, the first drag item appears when the slide loads. The next drag item only appears once the first item has been dragged. If you select this option, click the **Browse** button to bring up a dialog box letting you designate in what order the drag items should appear.

Drop Target Options

Snap dropped items...: This option and associated menu let you choose how the objects behave when released in the drop target.

- **Tile**: Objects are arranged so that they don't overlap. If there isn't enough space, objects may extend beyond the drop target.

- **Stack Random**: Objects are placed randomly in the target area.

- **Stack Offset**: Items are lined up to the top-left corner of the drop area, with each one slightly lower and to the right.

- **Snap to Center**: The drag items snap to the middle of the drop target. If there is more than one item per drop target, they overlap.

- **Free**: Objects stay where they are dropped.

Allow only one item in each drop target: Check this box if you only want to allow one item in each drop target. With this option selected, if the student tries to drag an item into a target that is already occupied, it goes back to its original position. The student must remove the item from the drop target before putting a different one there.

Feedback

You can set up triggers and states that change the appearance of drag items once they are over a certain drop area. Check this box if you don't want to show those states while the question is being answered, but rather wait until the student submits the answer.

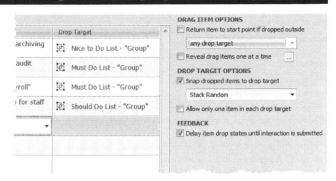

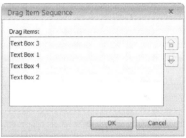

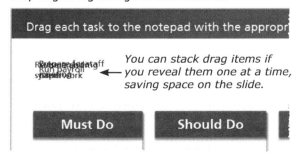

DESIGN TIP

What are the advantages of revealing drag items one at a time?

A drag-and-drop question can become very cluttered when you have to leave space for all of the drag items at their starting point and then have drop targets big enough to hold them all.

You can stack drag items if you reveal them one at a time, saving space on the slide.

You can also use this option if you'd rather not have the student see all the drag items at once, but instead consider and act on them one at a time.

Freeform Text Entry and Hotspot

The question editor for the freeform text entry and hotspot questions are identical to the text entry and hotspot questions on the **Graded** tab.

The main reason you might use the freeform version instead is if you already have a slide that you want to convert to a question. For example, you may already have a slide with the matrix shown on the right. By using the **Convert to Freeform** option (see next page), you can add the question elements to the slides, such as asking students to click on the task they would perform first.

Paired Comparison

Review vendor bids	✓✓
Revise archiving system	
Prepare for staff meeting	✓✓✓
Submit audit paperwork	✓✓✓✓
Write performance evaluations	✓

Click to add text

Existing slide

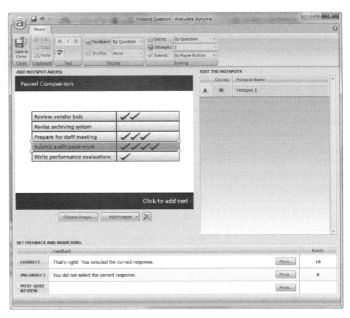

Slide converted to a freeform hotspot question

Convert to Freeform

You've already learned how to create a freeform question from the **Insert Slides** dialog box. You can also convert an existing slide to a freeform question.

To convert a slide to a freeform question:

1. Go to the **Insert** tab.
2. Click the **Convert to Freeform** button.
3. Select the question type you want.
4. Click the **OK** button.
5. Set up the question as described on the previous pages.

BRIGHT IDEA

To switch a freeform question slide back to a regular slide, click the **Remove Freeform** button that appears where the **Convert to Freeform** button used to be.

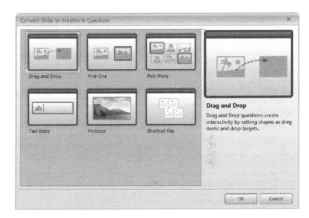

Freeform Shortcut Key Question

There is one freeform question option that is not available from the **Insert Slides** dialog box. You can only access it using the **Convert to Freeform** option.

Question Editor

- Click in the text field at the top and type the keystroke or keystroke combination that is considered correct.
- To change the keystroke, simply click in the field and type a different keystroke.

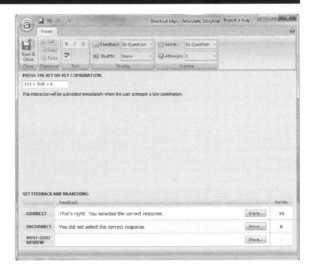

Edit a Question in the Question Editor

To return to the question editor to edit a question, click the **Edit** button just above the **Triggers** panel. **(A)**

When you are done, click the **Save & Close** button in the question editor. **(B)**

If you don't want to save your changes, click the **File** button in the question editor, and select **Cancel**. **(C)**

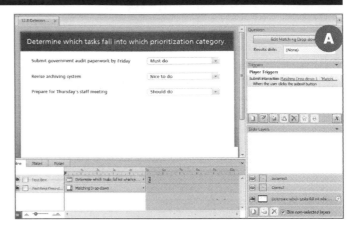

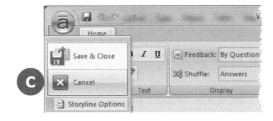

Modifying Questions in Slide View

The question editor isn't the only way you can add and modify question content. You can do it right on the slide as well.

A slide with a question can be treated much like any other slide. You can add objects, media, layers, states, and triggers. For example, you may want to create a scenario and don't want to put it all in the **Enter the Question** field in the question editor. You don't have to—you can just put it in a text box on the slide itself.

You can also add, delete, edit, format, and reposition the question elements from the form.

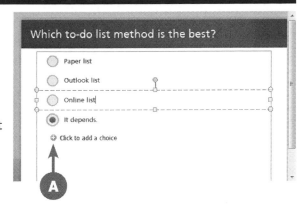

- To add a new question element (such as a new option to a multiple-choice question), just select any question element, and then click the green plus button that appears. **(A)**

- To delete a question element, select it on the slide and press the **Delete** key on your keyboard.

- To change which option is considered correct, select/de-select the radio button or check box for that option.

- To edit a question element, treat it like any other object of that type. For example, click in a text box to change the text on a multiple-choice option, go to the **Format** tab to change the color of a radio button, etc.

- There are some elements you can't change on the slide, such as changing the pairing of a matching question. You can go back to the question editor to do that.

TIME SAVER

In **Slide View**, you can copy and paste question items (such as the options in a multiple-choice question). Simply select the item on the slide, and use the buttons on the **Home** tab or **Ctrl** + **X**, **C**, and **V**.

Question Options

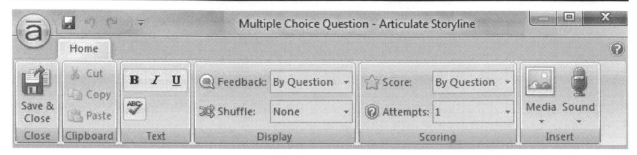

The **Home** tab in the question editor provides a number of formatting and logic options. The menu varies slightly for certain question types.

Clipboard and Text

The tools in these two sections let you cut, copy, paste, and format text in the question editor. You can also make changes like these (and more) in **Slide** view.

Feedback

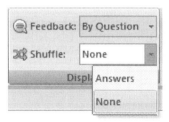

- **None**: Choose this option if you don't want feedback messages for your question. This is the default for survey questions.

- **By Question**: For graded and freeform questions, this means you can enter one message if the student gets the question correct and one message if the student gets the question incorrect. For survey questions, you can set up a single message that displays, regardless of what the student answers.

- **By Choice**: Some question types (such as multiple choice) let you set up feedback based on each choice. This means you can show separate feedback if the student selects the first choice or the second choice or the third choice.

Shuffle

Some questions (such as multiple choice) let you shuffle the choices. This means that the choices appear in a different random order for each student. Some question choices *require* shuffling (such as matching and sequence), in which case, this menu is disabled.

Score

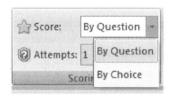

- **By Question**: Just as with feedback, you can assign a point value for a correct answer and another point value for an incorrect answer.

- **By Choice**: Certain question types (such as multiple choice) let you assign a different point value for each individual option. For example, you might award 10 points for the best answer and 5 points for a partially correct answer.

This field is disabled for survey questions.

Attempts

By default, questions have one attempt. From this drop-down menu, you can provide more than one attempt. When you select 2–10, the student gets the "incorrect" message if he or she answers the question wrong. However, the question is not actually counted as incorrect until the last attempt has been used up.

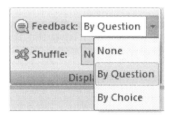

Question Options (cont'd)

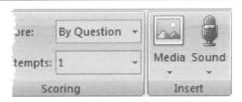

Media and Sound

Adding pictures, sound, and video from these menus is the same as adding them on the slide itself.

Submit

Hotspot questions have an additional field in the **Scoring** section, indicating when the question scores.

- **By Player Button**: The question is graded when the student clicks the **Submit** button—either the one in the player or one that you add yourself.

- **On Click**: The question is graded as soon as the student clicks anywhere on the slide.

- **On Double Click**: The question is graded as soon as the student double-clicks anywhere on the slide.

- **On Right Click**: The question is graded as soon as the student right-clicks anywhere on the slide.

Require

Survey questions have an extra option in the **Display** section. You can indicate if students can skip the survey question or if they must answer it before continuing.

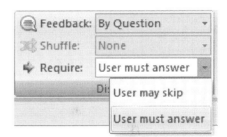

Feedback, Scoring, and Branching

Question feedback appears to the student on a slide layer. Because of this, you have a lot of flexibility as to how the feedback appears. The layers are configured based on the question options you set (see previous two pages). For example, if you allow more than one attempt, you will have a "try again" layer. If you have different feedback for each question choice, there will be a layer for each of those feedback options.

There are three ways to enter your feedback. You can:

- Enter feedback in the main window of the question editor.
- Enter feedback in a pop-up window from the question editor, which gives you a few additional formatting and logic choices.
- Enter feedback on the slide layer itself, giving you the most control over how it looks.

Scoring is done through the question editor. As you learned on the last page, you can set up scoring for each question, and with some question types, for each answer.

Branching lets you take students to a particular slide based on how they answered the question. This is useful if you want to create branching scenarios or use a separate slide for feedback, rather than the standard layer option.

Enter Feedback and Scoring in the Question Editor

For question-level feedback and scoring:

- Type your feedback in the **Correct** and **Incorrect** fields. **(A)**
- Click in the **Points** column for the **Correct** and **Incorrect** fields, and type the number of points the question is worth if right. **(B)**

For answer-level feedback and scoring, remember first to select the **By Choice** option from the **Feedback** and/or **Scoring** menus at the top. Then:

- Type your feedback in the **Feedback** column for each choice. **(C)**
- Click in the **Points** column and enter the number of points that each option is worth. **(D)**

Post-quiz review feedback shows up in a small caption in the bottom corner of the slide if you give the students the option to review the quiz. **(E)** To enter feedback in this caption, type your text in the **Post-Quiz Review** field. **(F)**

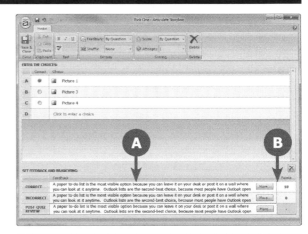

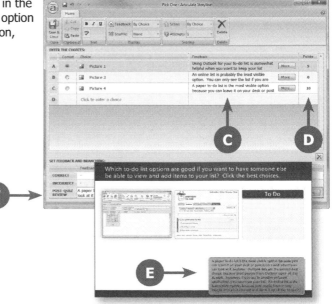

Enter Feedback and Branching in the Question Editor

If you click the **More** button **(A)** in any of the feedback fields, a dialog box comes up with additional options.

Formatting Text

If nothing else, this dialog box gives you a little more room to work, which might make it easier to type and edit your text. You can also use the **Bold**, **Italics**, and **Underline** buttons to add some simple formatting. (You can do more advanced formatting by going to the slide layer.)

Adding Audio

Use the **Audio** pane to add audio to your feedback, such as voiceover narration or sound effects. (You can also add audio by going to the slide layer.)

 Audio, p. 83

Setting up Branching

After getting feedback, students are taken, by default, to the next slide in the project, regardless of how they answer the question. If you'd like them to go to different slides based on how they answered the question, select the slide you want them to go to from the **Branching** drop-down menu. (You can also change the branching from the feedback layers on the slide—see next page.)

For example, in a branching scenario shown to the right, you would click the **More** button in the **Incorrect** feedback field on slide 3, and set the branching to go to slide 4. Then you'd click the **More** button in the **Correct** field, and set the branching to go to slide 5.

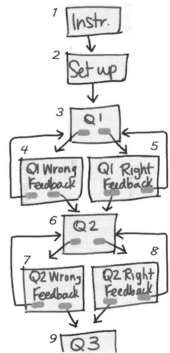

Planning diagram for a branching scenario

Feedback Layers

Layers are added to the slides based on the way you configured your question feedback. The appropriate layer displays based on how the students answered the question. Your layers might include:

- Correct.
- Incorrect (one layer if you chose question-level feedback, one per choice for choice-level feedback).
- Review.

You can manage these slide layers much like any slide layer. For example, you can:

- Format the existing text.
- Add other objects, such as more text boxes, shapes, images, etc.
- Add media.
- Adjust objects in the **Timeline**.
- Change the trigger on the **Continue** button to change the branching.

Layers, p. 106

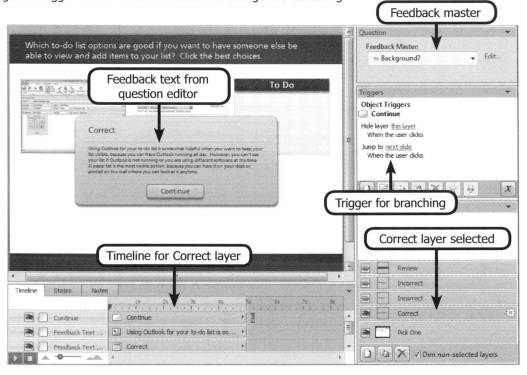

Apply a Different Feedback Master

Feedback slides, just like regular slides, are based on a master. You can create your own feedback masters and apply them to your slides. This lets you customize the look of your feedback without having to format each slide individually.

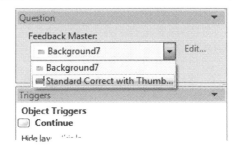

To change which feedback master is applied:

1. Select the slide you want to work with.
2. Select the layer you want to change.
3. Click the **Feedback Master** drop-down menu.
4. Select the master you want.

Create/Modify a Feedback Master

Feedback masters are very similar to regular slide masters. You can modify an existing master or layout, create a new master, or add a new layout to a master family.

Slide Masters, p. 31

To edit an existing master or layout:

1. Go to the **View** tab.
2. Click the **Feedback Master** button.
3. Select the master or layout you want to modify.
4. Make your changes.
5. Click **Close Master View**.

To create a new master:

1. Click the **Insert Master Slide** button.

When you add a new master, the placeholders for the heading, feedback text, and **Continue** button are already on the slide for you.

To create a new slide layout:

1. Select the master slide you want to base the layout on.
2. Click the **Insert Layout** button.

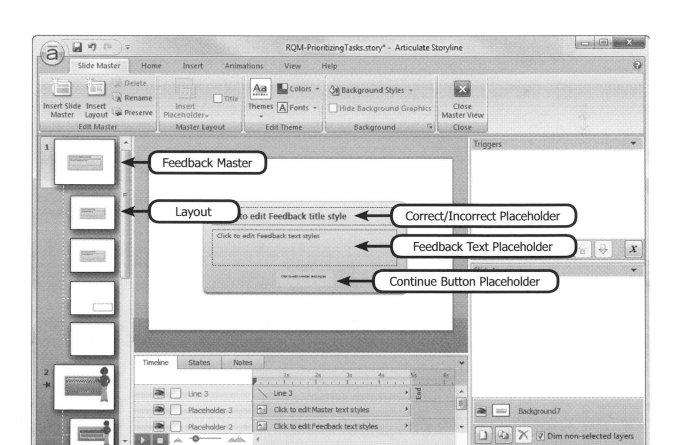

Question Banks

Question banks are groups of questions that "live" within your project, separate from any individual slide. Having questions organized into banks makes it easy to reuse them and also lets you set up randomization. For example, you might want to:

- Use the same questions in both a pre-test and a post-test.
- Show different questions to each student, or show them in a different order to help reduce "creative sharing" of answers.
- Give students the chance to try a quiz again, presenting the questions in a different order the second time through.

Working with question banks is a three-step process.

Create a Question Bank

To create a new question bank:

1. In **Story View**, click the **Question Banks** button.
2. Select **Create Question Bank**.
3. Type a name for the question bank.
4. Click the **OK** button.

 DESIGN TIP

If you will only be pulling in some (not all) of the questions, set up a different bank for each objective. That way, you know that all objectives will be adequately covered.

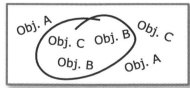

Three questions pulled randomly from one bank—not all objectives are covered

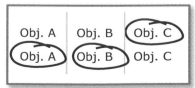

One question pulled randomly from each of three banks—all objectives are covered

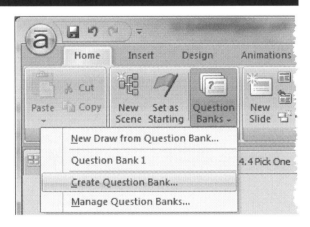

Open an Existing Question Bank

When you create or open a question bank, it opens up in a tab like a regular slide would.

To open an existing bank of questions:
1. From **Story View**, click the **Question Banks** button.
2. Select the question bank you want to open.

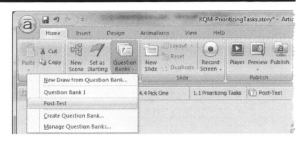

Add a Question to a Bank

To create a new question in an open question bank:
1. Click the **Graded Question** or **Survey Question** button. **(A)**
2. Select the question type you want. **(B)**
3. Click the **Insert** button.
4. Set up your question as normal.
5. Click the **Save & Close** button.

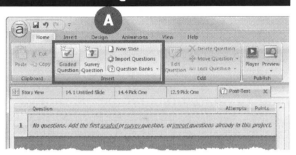

To import a question already in the project into a question bank:
1. Click the **Import Questions** button. **(A)**
2. Select the question(s) you want to import. **(C)**
3. Click the **OK** button.

Options
- In the **Import from** drop-down menu, indicate if you want to import from a regular slide (**Story**) or another question bank.

- In the **Import** drop-down menu, indicate if you want to copy the questions (meaning leave the originals where they are) or move the questions (meaning remove the questions from where they are).

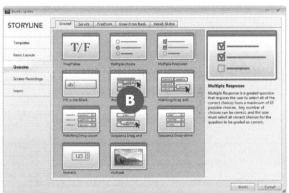

To insert a blank slide into an open question bank:
1. Click the **New Slide** button.

 DESIGN TIP

Blank slides are useful if you want instructions or a scenario at the beginning of a set of questions.

 CAUTION

Remember that adding a question to a question bank does not put the question in your published project. You still need to pull questions from the bank into the project.

Draw Question-Bank Questions Into a Project

To draw question-bank questions into a project:

1. From **Story View**, click the **Question Banks** drop-down button.
2. Select **New Draw from Question Bank**.

——— or ———

1. From the **Home** tab, click the **Insert Slides** button.
2. Click the **Quizzing** tab.
3. Click the **Draw from Bank** tab.

—— from there ——

4. In the **Question Bank** field, select the bank you want to draw from.
5. Check or uncheck **Draw questions randomly**.
6. If drawing questions randomly, select the number of questions you want to draw.
7. Change the options you want (see below).
8. Click the **Insert** button.

Options

- If you do not check the randomization check box, all questions will appear in the order listed.

- If you check the randomization check box and include all the questions, all the questions will be pulled into the project and will appear in a different order each time for each student.

- If you check the randomization option and select only some of the questions, only those questions will be pulled in and will appear in a different order each time for each student.

- If you are not including all of the questions from the bank, use the **Include in Shuffle** drop-down menu to manage which slides appear in the project.

  - **Randomly**: This is the default. The question gets no special weight or consideration.

  - **Never**: Select this option for questions that you do not want pulled into the project.

  - **Always**: Select this option for questions that should always be pulled into the project, such as instruction slides or an extremely important question. For example, if you only pull 5 out of 12 questions, any question set to **Always** will be included in those 5 questions every time.

- **Lock Question**: To lock a question either to another question or to the beginning/end of the questions, select the question, click the **Lock Question** button, and select the lock option you want.

- **Move Question**: Click and drag the questions to rearrange them. Or you can select the question, click the **Move Question** button, and select **Up** or **Down**.

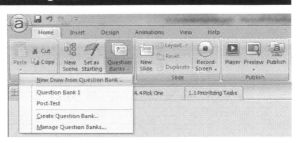

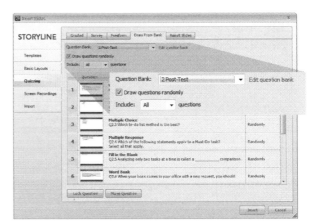

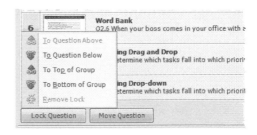

 BRIGHT IDEA

Locking questions is useful if you plan to randomize them, but want to keep certain slides together (such as a scenario slide and its corresponding question) or keep it at the beginning or end (such as instructions).

Pull Question-Bank Questions Into a Project (cont'd)

When you draw question-bank questions into a project, they all appear on a single placeholder slide, regardless of how many questions you are pulling.

If you view the placeholder slide in **Slide** view, you will not see the individual questions. Instead, there are two options: **Click to view the slide draw** and **Click to view the question bank**.

Bringing up the slide draw takes you back to the **Draw Questions from Bank** dialog box. Here you can change the settings from when you set up the draw, such as how many questions to include. Changes made here only affect how the questions are brought into this particular project.

Bringing up the question bank takes you back to the same view as when you added the questions. Changes made here affect the main question pool.

Viewing the slide draw

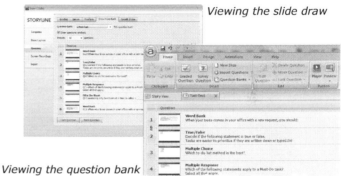

Viewing the question bank

Manage Questions in a Bank

You can manage the questions in a bank using the tools on the **Home** tab and the right-click menu.

To edit a question:

1. Double-click the question.

—— or ——

1. Select the question.
2. Click the **Edit Question** button.

To rearrange questions:

1. Click and drag the question to where you want it.

—— or ——

1. Select the question you want to move.
2. Click the **Move Question** button.
3. Select **Up** or **Down**.

To lock a question:

1. Select the question you want to lock.
2. Click the **Lock Question** button.
3. Select the locking option you want.

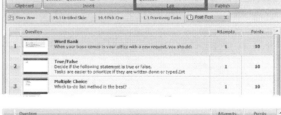

To delete a question:

1. Select the question.
2. Click the **Delete Question** button.

Manage Question Banks

To manage question banks:

1. From **Story View**, click the **Question Banks** button.
2. Select **Manage Question Banks**.
3. Select the bank you want to work with.
4. Make the changes you want using the buttons at the bottom of the **Question Bank Manager**.
5. Click the **Close** button.

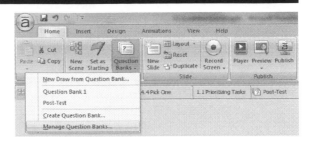

Create New · Edit (Open) · Duplicate · Rename · Delete

BRIGHT IDEA

You can import individual questions and whole question banks using the import feature. Select the Storyline option when importing from the **Insert Slides** dialog box, and select the question slides you want to import.

Importing Slides p. 24

Results Slides

When you add a question to a slide, it is a standalone question with no relation to other questions. If you want to group slides together to have cumulative scoring and pass/fail logic, then all you have to do is set up a results slide. Results slides basically turn a group of independent questions into a scored quiz. A results slide can include one, some, or all of the questions in your story. You can have multiple results slides in a story, and you can even have a results slide that combines the scores from other results slides. When publishing your course, you can pick one of your results slides to set completion status and be sent to a learning management system.

 Publishing, ch. 15

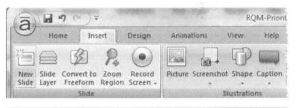

Create a Results Slide

To create a results slide:

1. Go to the **Insert** tab from **Slide** view or the **Home** tab from **Story View**.
2. Click the **New Slide** button.
3. Click the **Quizzing** tab.
4. Click the **Results Slide** tab.
5. Select the results slide type you want.
6. Click the **Insert** button.
7. Configure the options based on the result slide type. (See next three pages.)
8. Click the **OK** button.

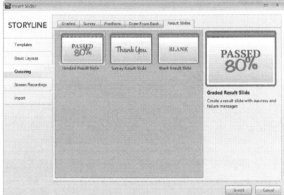

Graded Results Slide

Results Tab

Calculate results for: Indicate if you want the results to come from individual questions that you select or from combining results from other results slides.

Results from Selected Questions

Question: Select the questions you want to include in this results slide.

Passing Score: Enter the percentage of the total available points the student must earn to pass the quiz.

End quiz after: Check this box if you want a timed test. When you select this option, the following options become available:

> **Start timer**: Indicate if you want the timer to start with the first question or with the first slide. (This is only relevant if the first slide isn't a question, such as an instructions slide or the details of a scenario.)

> **Timer format**: Indicate how you want the timer to be displayed, if at all. Choices are:

- **Elapsed out of total**, such as 1:25 out of 5:00
- **Do not show time**
- **Elapsed**, meaning how much time has passed
- **Remaining**, meaning how much time is left

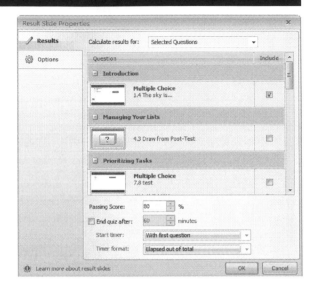

Results from Other Results

Results Slide: Select the results slides you want to combine for this results slide.

User must pass each quiz: If you select this option, the student must pass each individual quiz (according to the settings for that quiz) in order to pass this "master quiz."

Combine points from each quiz: If you select this option, it does not matter whether the student passes or fails the individual quizzes. Instead, all the points are combined, and the student must earn the overall score you enter here.

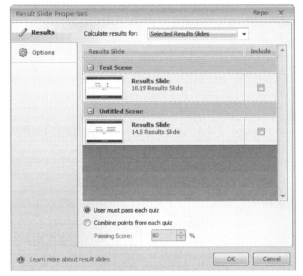

DESIGN TIP

A results slide is much like any other slide, and you can make formatting and logic changes to it accordingly.

Graded Results Slide

Options Tab

Show User's Score

The user's score is included by default on results slides. Uncheck this box if you do not want it included.

Show Passing Score

The passing percentage is included by default. Uncheck this box if you do not want it displayed.

Allow User to Review Quiz

The results screen contains a **Review Quiz** button that takes students back through the quiz question by question. Uncheck this box if you don't want students to be able to review the quiz. The post-quiz review includes:

- Any text you entered in the **Post-Quiz Review** field in the question editor.
- Correct/incorrect status at the bottom of the slide.
- Correct/incorrect responses on the slide, if the **Show correct/incorrect responses when reviewing** check box is checked. Uncheck this box if you don't want the students to see the correct/incorrect answers.

Allow User to Print Results

If you check this box, a **Print Results** button is added to the results slide. When the student clicks this button, a new browser window opens with a printable summary of the quiz results. The students will need to use the print function in the browser to actually print the results.

Prompt the User for Their Name Before Printing

If you are including the print function, you can check this box to have a dialog box come up, asking for the student's name. When a student enters his or her name in this dialog box, the name is included in the printable results.

Allow User to Retry Quiz

If you check this box, a **Retry Quiz** button is added to the results slide. This button clears the answers and takes the student back to the beginning of the quiz. When you allow retries, the earlier attempts do not count against the student's score.

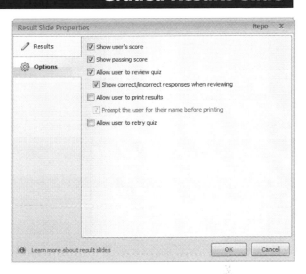

BRIGHT IDEA

Some of these options are not available on a combined results slide.

Results slide with all options turned on

Review mode showing correct/ incorrect responses and review text

Printable results page with student name

Survey Results Slide

A survey results slide is much like a graded results slide, with the following exceptions.

Results Tab

Surveys don't have passing scores, so that option is disabled on the **Results** tab.

Options Tab

On the **Options** tab, the options for showing the user's score and the passing score are unavailable, since there are no scores in a survey.

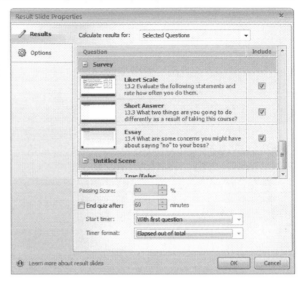

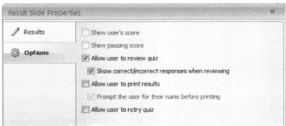

Blank Results Slide

The **Results** tab for a blank results slide is identical to a graded results slide.

The **Options** tab for a blank results slide has the same options, but the defaults are different, with most of the features turned off.

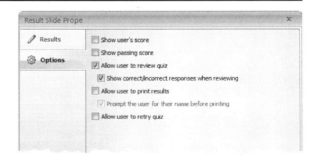

POWER TIP

Blank results slides are most useful when you want to set up your own logic. You can use quiz-related variables to set the slide up however you want.

Quiz-Related Variables

When you create a quiz by adding a results slide, new variables are added to your project. These variables are used in results slides.

 Variables, p. 133

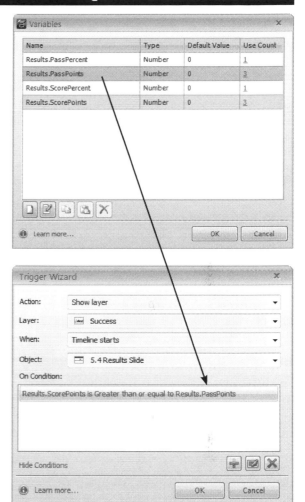

Quiz-Related Action Triggers

In addition to the action triggers you learned about in chapter 10, there are some additional triggers that relate to quizzes and questions. These variables are already used in the standard quiz logic. Because they are available to you, you can use them to create your own logic instead of using the standard logic. For example, you could:

- Create a submit button for a question instead of using the one that comes with the course player.

- Create your own buttons on a results slide, rather than using the default buttons.

 Actions, ch. 10

Submit Interaction

If there is a question on the slide, use this action to grade the question. This action is used on the player's **Submit** button.

Submit Results

Use this action to grade the overall quiz. This action automatically runs when a results slide starts.

Review Results

Use this action to take the student back through the quiz in review mode. This action is used on the **Review Quiz** button.

Reset Results

Use this action to return all the related questions back to their unanswered state. This action is used on the default **Retry Quiz** button.

Print Results

Use this button to bring up a new browser window with a summary of the quiz results. This action is used on the **Print Results** button.

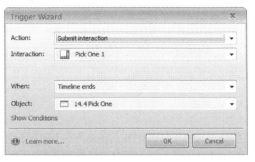

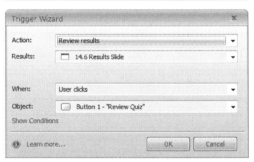

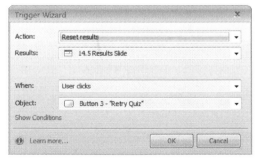

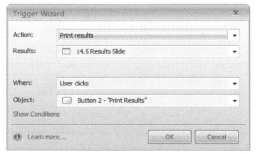

POWER TIP

In this chapter, you've learned how to create questions and quizzes using the standard options available in the various editors and dialog boxes. You can also use the building blocks you've learned about in previous chapters to add your own logic to a question or build questions from scratch.

Remember that you can:

- Add buttons, check boxes, radio buttons, hotspots, and data entry boxes to any slide.

- Turn just about any object into a drag item or drop target to make your own drag-and-drop activity.

- Add triggers to any of these objects to show layers for feedback, jump to different slides for branching, or add points to custom-created variables to keep score.

- Add extra logic to correct/incorrect layers.

- Use the question editor but then add extra triggers or conditions to the existing logic.

This process is more manual, which may be an advantage (a little more design flexibility) or a disadvantage (you don't get the feedback logic).

Example of a question from the question editor with extra logic that turns it into a game

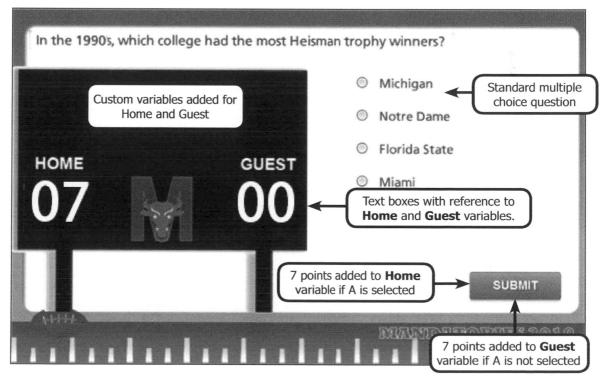

Notes

Screen Recordings

Introduction

Storyline comes with a powerful screen recording process that lets you capture the steps you record on your computer and then play it back in your project as a movie, a step-by-step demonstration, a "try-me" guided practice, or a "test me" assessment.

You can record your screen once and then add the recording to your project using any of the four modes, add annotations such as captions and zoom areas, edit individual screen shots, and even export the movie for use elsewhere.

Notes

Preparing for Your Recording

To prepare for a screen recording session, you'll need to make a few decisions.

❏ **Do you want to create a new project from the recording or include it in an existing project?** This will help you determine what procedure to use. But don't worry, you can change your mind later and bring a stand-alone capture into an existing project or vice-versa.

❏ **How big do you want to make the recording?** You'll need to decide what size to make the recording area. You'll need to consider the student's computer resolution as well as how big the software application window needs to be to show everything you want to show.

❏ **What parts of the software application do you want to include/exclude?** For example, in a web application, do you need to show the browser toolbars?

❏ **Do you want to narrate as you capture, or import/record audio after the capture?** Recording narration while you capture is quicker, but you might prefer to record narration later so that you can write and approve a script, use someone else to record the narration, or simply so you don't have to do two things at once.

❏ **What software preparation is necessary before recording?** Think of the cooking shows where the onions are already chopped and the salt already measured. What steps or set-up might you need to do in the software before recording?

You'll also need to make some important instructional design decisions. You generally don't have to act on these decisions until after you are done recording, but it's a good idea to know the answers before you get started.

❏ **Do you want the student to watch the steps or try them?** You'll record the capture the same way regardless, but knowing this may affect what you choose to record.

If the students will be trying the steps themselves:

❏ **How will you communicate the task your students need to accomplish?** Will you give them an audio introduction stating the scenario? Will you want captions that describe each step?

❏ **How detailed should instructions and feedback be?** Should instructions and feedback for an incorrect action be general or specific? Should the instruction/feedback point directly to the feature they need to use? If asking students to try again, should they be given help?

There will be additional choices to make as you are selecting which mode to use and which features for that mode you should turn on and off. You'll learn more about these features throughout the rest of the chapter.

 **BRIGHT IDEA**

Before capturing, be sure to turn off anything that might bring up an unwanted pop-up message during your recording session, such as Outlook or instant messaging.

Create a Screen Recording

The initial part of this procedure varies based on whether you are creating a new project from the recording or adding it to an existing project. The rest of the procedure is the same from there.

To create a screen recording:

1. From the **Welcome Screen**, click the **Record screen** link.

——— or ———

1. Click the **Record Screen** button on the **Home** tab of **Story View** or the **Insert** tab on a page.

2. Set the size and position of the recording frame. (See below.)

3. Set the audio options. (See next page.)

4. Set the recording options. (See next page.)

5. Click the **Record** button.

6. Perform the steps in the software.

7. Click the **Done** button. (The **Cancel** button becomes a **Done** button once recording starts.)

8. Configure the settings in the **Insert Slides** dialog box (see page 189).

9. Click the **Insert** button.

Recording Window Size and Position

The recording frame **(A)** marks the boundaries of what will get recorded. You have the following options for setting the size and position of the recording frame:

- Click and drag the handles on the recording frame to change the size. **(B)** Drag a corner handle to keep the frame in the same aspect ratio as your story size. Drag a side handle to change the proportion.

- Click and drag the gray box in the middle of the recording frame **(C)** to reposition the frame.

- Click the **Recording frame options** menu, and select a pre-set size.

- Click the **Recording frame options** menu, and select **Select a Window (D)** to have Storyline detect the window. Move your mouse around the different areas of your screen, and watch the red recording frame. Click your mouse when it is around the section you want.

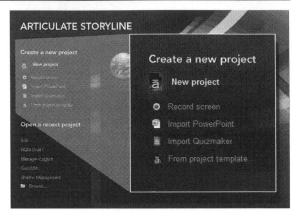

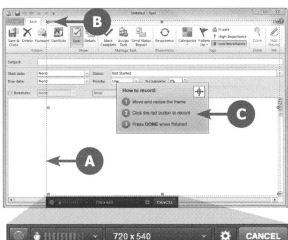

Record | Microphone | Recording frame options | Settings | Cancel/Done

Create a Screen Recording (cont'd)

Audio Options

Click the microphone pop-up menu **(A)** to select the microphone you want to use to record audio, or select **No Audio** if you don't want to record audio while capturing.

Recording Options

Click the settings button **(B)** to change recording settings.

Shortcuts

By default, the keyboard shortcuts shown to the right can be used during your capture session. If you prefer to use different keystrokes, simply type the keystroke you want in each of the fields.

Sound Recording

- The **Microphone** field gives you the same choices as the pop-up menu described above. Either select a microphone from the list, or uncheck the box if you don't want to record audio.

- Use the **Speakers** field if you want to record system sounds during your capture.

Options

- **Move new windows into recording area**: If you are recording a procedure that involves pop-up windows, such as a dialog box, there's a chance that the dialog box will appear outside of the recording frame. Check this box if you want Storyline to move any new windows inside the recording frame for you.

- **System tray icon**: If this box is checked, a small icon appears in your system tray **(C)** while you are recording. You can double-click the icon to stop the capture. Uncheck this box if you don't want the icon to appear. For example, if your capture includes the system tray, you might not want the icon to show.

Commands During Capture

During your capture, the recording toolbar changes, giving you different tools. Click the **Pause** button to pause the recording (which brings back the **Record** button to click when you are ready to resume), click the trash can icon to stop and delete the recording while still keeping the recording frame up, or click the **Done** button to finish the recording. You can also press the **Escape** key on your keyboard or double-click the system tray icon to stop the recording.

CAUTION

Type carefully! Typing is one of the few things you cannot edit after recording.

Playback Modes

Storyline captures and saves a full video recording of your capture. However, you can add it to your project in one or more of the four different playback modes.

Video	View Mode	Try Mode	Test Mode
Additional objects, such as captions and shapes, can be added and timed.			
Students watch the recording.		Students perform the steps themselves.	
The recording plays as a single video on a single slide. Actions show in real time.	Each action is converted to its own slide.		
	Slides and slide elements can be edited.		
	Automatic captions describe the steps.		Slide advances when the student performs the step properly or reaches the designated number of attempts. Student can have more than one attempt. Steps are graded as questions. Results can be tracked or used for conditional logic.
	Caption text is used as the slide title.		
	Captions are available in 11 languages.		
	Captions are designed to instruct. Slides advance automatically. Slides can include animated mouse movements. Slides can include a highlight box to highlight the step being performed.	Captions are designed as hints, showing up either automatically or when the student hovers over the target area. Slide advances when the student performs a step properly.	
		Correct and incorrect feedback can be added.	

DESIGN TIP

How do you decide which mode to use?

- First, decide if you want the student to watch or perform the steps themselves.
- If the student will be watching, decide if the procedure is simple enough to use as captured or if it is likely to need some fine-tuning and editing.
- If the students will be practicing, decide if you want to give them hints or ask them to remember the steps on their own without help.

Keep in mind that you can modify individual settings in case you want a hybrid approach, such as providing hints and tracking results.

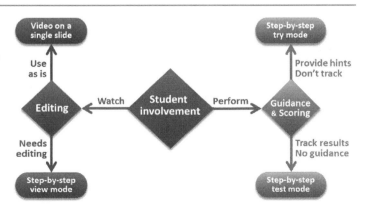

Insert the Recording Into Your Project

When you are finished recording, the **Insert Slides** dialog box appears, giving you options about how you want the recording to appear in your project. Your recording is captured as a video. However, you do not have to insert it as a video.

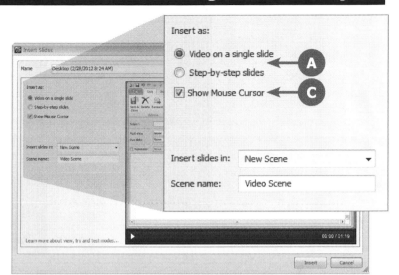

Insert As

Here you select which mode you want to use. Select the radio button for video or step-by-step. **(A)** If you choose step-by-step, a drop-down menu appears letting you select view, try, or test mode. **(B)**

Video Mode Options

If you choose the video mode, you can indicate if you want to show the mouse cursor in the video. Uncheck the **Show Mouse Cursor** box if you don't want to include the mouse. **(C)**

View Mode Options

If you choose the view mode, a **View Mode Options** link **(D)** appears with options for what to include in the capture. **(E)** These settings apply to the entire recording. Once the slides are inserted, you can change the settings on a slide-by-slide basis.

- **Language for captions**: Choose from 11 different languages for captions and slide titles.

- **Add text captions**: By default, captions are added to describe the steps being performed. Uncheck the box if you don't want them.

- **Show Mouse Cursor**: Your mouse cursor appears on each slide as a moving animation. Uncheck the box if you don't want to include the mouse.

- **Indicate clicks with highlight**: When the mouse clicks in the recording, a small blue highlight appears to help emphasize the click. Uncheck this box if you don't want to include it.

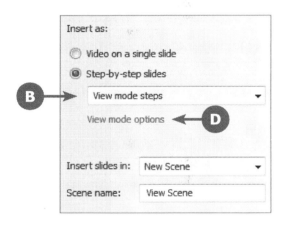

Insert Options

You can choose to either insert the slide(s) in a new scene (and give it a name) or select from an existing scene.

 BRIGHT IDEA

If you don't like the settings you chose, you can always re-insert the recording with new settings.

 Re-Insert a Recording, p. 200

Insert the Recording Into Your Project (cont'd)

Try Mode Options

If you've selected **Try Mode Steps**, you get a link for the **Try Mode Options**.

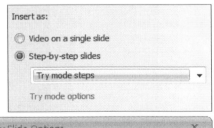

- **Language for Captions**: Select from the 11 available languages for the hint captions and slide titles.

- **Show correct feedback**: By default, the students know they got the steps correct because they move on in the simulation. However, if you'd like to add correct feedback to each step, check this box.

- **Show hand cursor...**: In try mode, a hotspot appears over the area where the students are supposed to click. These hotspots have hint captions. By default, the student's mouse becomes a hand cursor when it is over the hotspot, letting the student know that it is a hotspot. Uncheck this button if you don't want that effect.

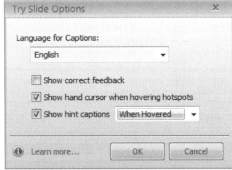

- **Show hint captions**: If you don't want to show hint captions, uncheck this box. If you do want captions, you can keep the default of **When Hovered**, meaning the caption shows when the student rolls over the target area, or **Always**, which means the caption is visible based on its timing in the **Timeline**.

Test Mode Options

If you've selected **Test Mode Steps**, you get a link for the **Test Mode Options**.

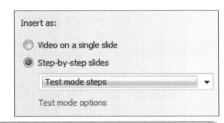

- **Show correct feedback**: By default, the students know they got the steps correct because they move on in the simulation. However, if you'd like to add correct feedback to each step, check this box.

- **Show incorrect feedback**: By default, a feedback window appears if the student clicks anywhere other than the hotspot or types anything other than the acceptable text. Uncheck this box if you don't want to show incorrect feedback.

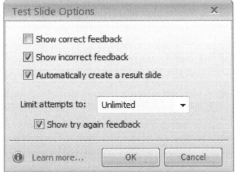

- **Automatically create a result slide**: Each hotspot or text entry box is actually a question. As such, Storyline can create a results slide giving the student a summary of their performance in the test. The test results can be tracked, used for completion status, or used for conditional logic.

- **Limit attempts to**: By default, the student must continue trying to perform the step correctly before moving on. If you want to limit the number of attempts the student needs to take before seeing the incorrect feedback and moving on, select that number from the drop-down list.

- **Show try again feedback**: By default, if you allow more than one attempt, Storyline includes a message telling the student the answer is incorrect and to try again. Uncheck this box if you don't want that message.

 CAUTION

- Be careful about adding correct feedback. For a 12-step procedure, 12 pop-up windows need to be read and closed. Seeing the simulation continue is often enough indication for them to know they got the answer correct.

- Unlimited attempts can be frustrating for a student who truly doesn't know what to do. Use this option carefully.

Managing a Video Slide

If you insert your recording as a movie, it works very much like any other movie. You can:

- Adjust the starting point in the **Timeline**.

- Resize and reposition the movie on the slide.

- Add other elements to the slide, such as captions, timed to the movie.

- Cut the end off of the movie by shortening the movie object in the **Timeline**.

- Change how the video plays (add controls, add actions, etc.).

- Use the **Options** tab to use the video management tools such as for adjusting volume or editing the video.

 Video, pp. 89–96

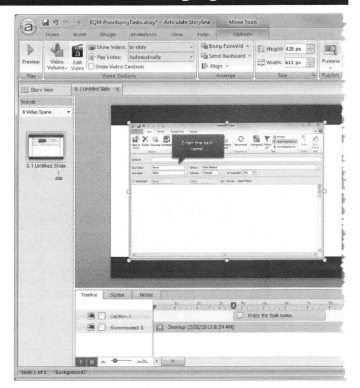

Managing View Mode Slides

When you insert a recording in view mode, Storyline turns each step into its own slide, with the caption text as the slide name **(A)**. Each slide contains a screen shot of the "before" state and a short animation showing the "after" state, such as a the appearance of a drop-down menu. **(B)** Based on your settings, the slides may contain captions **(C)**, mouse movements **(D)**, and highlight boxes **(E)**.

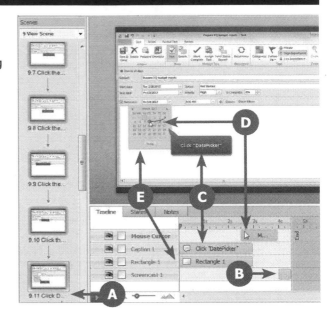

You can edit many aspects of these slides like you can with any slide. For example, you can:

- Delete slides.
- Add, edit, and delete captions.
- Add other elements, such as text boxes, arrows, and narration.
- Adjust the timing of the various on-screen elements.

Mouse Options

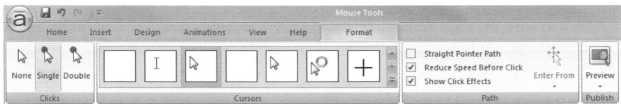

When you select the mouse, the **Mouse Tools: Format** tab appears.

Clicks

- **None**: Plays no sound when the mouse animation clicks.
- **Single**: Plays a click sound.
- **Double**: Plays a double-click sound.

Cursors: Storyline tries to show the same type of cursor that was used in your software during the recording. You can change the mouse appearance from the gallery.

Path: By default, mouse movements take a slightly curved path, slow down slightly before clicking, and show a small circle to indicate a mouse click. Check or uncheck any of these options in the **Path** section to change these options.

Enter From: Use this drop-down menu to indicate what direction you want the mouse to come from. If there is a mouse movement on the previous slide, this option is disabled, as the mouse will come from its position on the last slide.

BRIGHT IDEA

If you want to show a mouse movement on a slide that doesn't already have one, go to the **Insert** menu, and click the **Mouse** button.

POWER TIP

In addition to selecting from the cursor gallery, you can import your own. Storyline accepts cursor (**.cur**) and animated cursor (**.ani**) files.

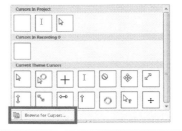

Action Fine Tuning

When you insert your screen recording in one of the step-by-step modes, the images are pulled from the video recording. In addition, many slides contain a short animation that mimics any animated effects such as typing, scrolling or dragging actions, panels or menus expanding or collapsing, etc. These animations are short video clips pulled from the original video.

With Action Fine Tuning, you can change which image is pulled for the slide and how any animations appear.

To fine tune an animation:
1. Right-click the slide.
2. Select **Action Fine Tuning**.
3. Make your changes.
4. Click **OK**.

Options

- To change the screen capture pulled for the slide (which also serves as the starting point for any animation), click and drag the green slider to the frame you want. **(A)** For more precise control, click the **Previous Frame** or **Next Frame** button until you are at the starting point you want.

- To change the end point of the animation, click and drag the white slider **(B)** to where you want it to end.

- To remove the animation completely, uncheck the **Show Animation** check box.

- To reset the screen capture and animation to their original settings, click the **Reset Original Timing** button.

 DESIGN TIP

Why might you want to fine tune an animation? Here are some possible reasons:

- There might be an unwanted tooltip showing **(C)**, and you want to pull the screen capture from before the tooltip appeared.

- You may want to remove the animation completely because it shows something you don't want to see. For example, if you made and fixed a typo while typing, you can remove the typing animation, showing the finished text only.

- You may want to remove the animation because you need to make edits to the underlying screen capture. For example, you may need to hide an employees name. You can do this in the static screen capture, but not in the animation.

- A hover effect in the software (such as a menu item glowing) shows up before the mouse arrives, and you want to change the screen capture so that the hover effect doesn't appear too soon.

Adding Zoom Regions

Zoom regions let you magnify certain portions of a step-by-step slide (or any slide, for that matter), making it easier for your student to see the features being discussed.

To add a zoom region:

1. Go to the **Insert** menu.

2. Click the **Zoom Region** button.

3. Resize and reposition the region as needed.

4. Adjust the timing of the region in the **Timeline** to zoom in and out when you want.

Options

- You can have multiple zoom regions on a single slide.

- When you put two zoom regions next to each other in the **Timeline**, it creates a panning effect.

- Zoom regions are locked at the same aspect ratio (height/width proportion) as the slide.

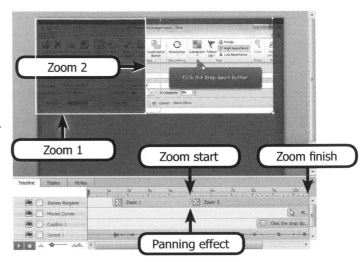

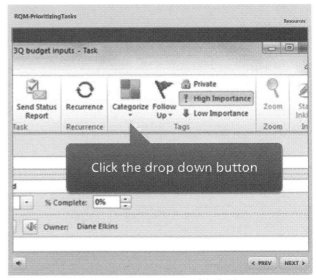

Zoom region 2 showing in published project.

Editing Try and Test Mode Slides

Remember that in Try mode and Test mode, the student performs the steps. To accomplish this, each slide is converted to an interactive slide, using hotspots for clicks and text entry boxes for typing.

The next four pages outline the specific elements used to create clicking and typing slides in Try mode and Test mode. Your slides may look slightly different based on what options you set.

You can use just about anything you learned up until this point in the book to edit these types of slides. For example, you can:

• Add objects such as captions, text boxes, shapes, etc. (See chapters 4 and 5.)

• Change the text, formatting, placement, and timing of captions, hotspots, and other objects. (See chapters 6 and 7.)

• Add audio narration. (See chapter 8.)

• Add mouse movements. (See page 192.)

• Change the text, formatting, and logic of the feedback layers. (See chapters 9 and 10.)

• Edit question settings such as number of attempts or feedback branching. (See chapter 12.)

• Fine tune the animations. (See page 193.)

In the end, you can treat your step-by-step slides like other slides in your project. And if you don't like the changes you've made, you can always re-insert the screen recording again.

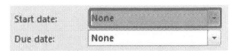

Format tab for captions

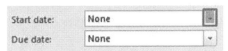

Hotspot as captured

Hotspot extended for greater accuracy

Multiple acceptable answers for text entry

Question logic for a test mode hotspot

Try Mode Slides: Clicks

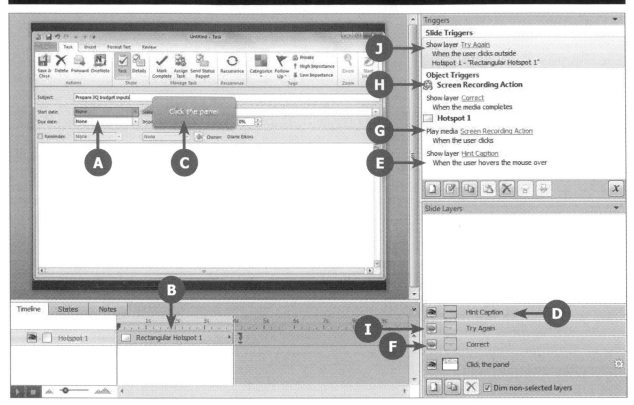

Remember that with Try mode, the student performs the steps and is not graded. To accomplish this, each slide is converted into an interactive slide, using hotspots for clicks and text entry box questions for typing. The following objects and actions are used for slides with a click action. Your slides may look slightly different based on what options you set.

A. Hotspot where the student needs to click to perform the step successfully

B. Main **Timeline** showing the hotspot

C. Hint caption

D. Hint caption layer (in **Show** mode)

E. Action showing the hint caption layer when the student hovers over the hotspot

F. Correct message layer

G. Action showing the animation if the student clicks the hotspot correctly. (The animation shows what happens next in the system when the step is performed correctly.)

H. Action showing the correct feedback layer when the animation is done playing

I. Try again message layer

J. Action showing the try again layer if the student clicks anywhere but the hotspot

 POWER TIP

You can add your own action triggers to create branching logic. For example, let's say that on slide 1, the student clicks the **File** menu. On slide 2, he or she clicks **Save As**. On slide 3, the **Save As** dialog box appears.

You can add another trigger to slide 1 that takes the student directly to slide 3 if the student presses **F12**.

Try Mode Slide: Text

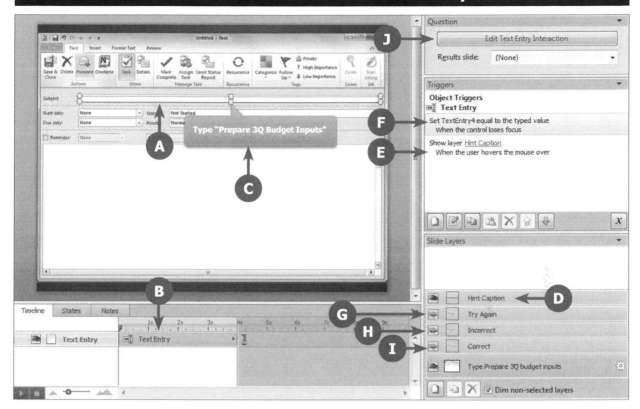

The following objects and actions are used for slides with a typing action. Your slides may look slightly different based on what options you set.

A. Text entry question where the student needs to type the correct text
B. Main **Timeline** showing the text entry question
C. Hint caption
D. Hint caption layer (in **Show** mode)
E. Action showing the hint caption layer when the student hovers over the text entry box
F. Action grading the question when the text entry box loses focus (clicks somewhere else after typing)
G. Try again message layer
H. Incorrect message layer
I. Correct message layer
J. Button to edit the question settings (showing the correct, incorrect, and try again layers, animation, etc.)

Test Mode Slides: Clicks

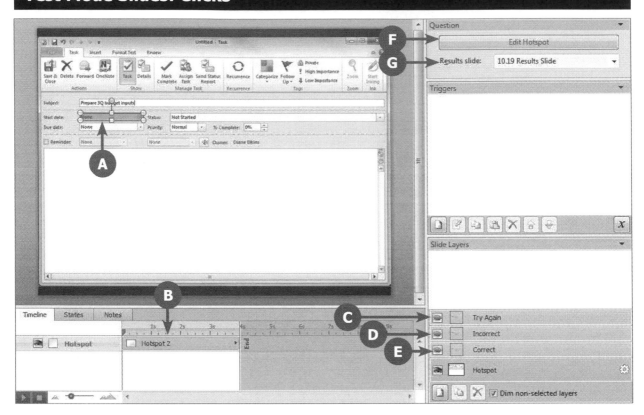

Remember that Test mode slides use scored question logic to have the students perform the test. Click actions in test mode use the hotspot question type, rather than the hotspot interactive object. The following objects and actions are used for test slides with a click action. Your slides may look slightly different based on what options you set.

A. Hotspot where the student needs to click to perform the step successfully

B. Main **Timeline** showing the hotspot

C. Try again message layer

D. Incorrect message layer

E. Correct message layer

F. Button to edit the hotspot question (showing the correct, incorrect, and try again layers, etc.)

G. Results slide used to track results

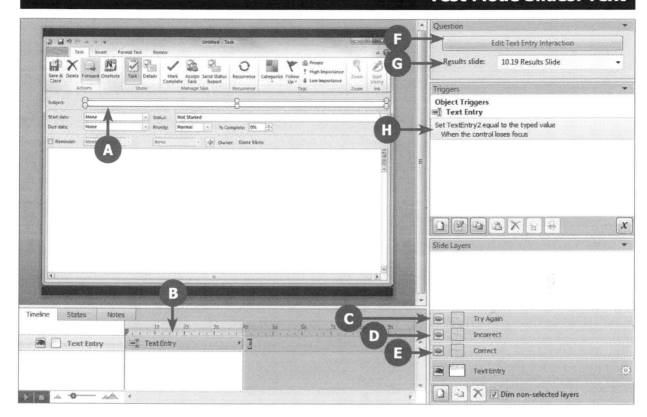

Typing slides are almost identical in Try mode and Test mode—both modes use the text entry question type. The main differences are that there is no hint caption, and a few of the question settings are different (awarding points, number of attempts, results slide, etc.) The following objects and actions are used for test slides with typing. Your slides may look slightly different based on what options you set.

A. Text entry question where the student needs to type the correct text

B. Main **Timeline** showing the text entry question

C. Try again message layer

D. Incorrect message layer

E. Correct message layer

F. Button to edit the hotspot question (showing the correct, incorrect, and try again layers, etc.)

G. Results slide used to track results

H. Action grading the question when the text entry box loses focus (clicks somewhere else after typing)

Re-Insert a Recording

Remember that your "raw" recording is stored with your **.story** file. This means you can go back to it at any time and re-insert the recording into your project. For example, you may not like the changes you've made and want to start over, or you want to include the recording in more than one mode.

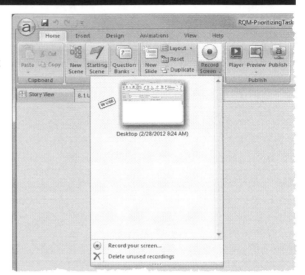

To re-insert a recording into the project:

1. Go to the **Insert** tab in a page view or the **Home** tab in **Story View**.

2. Click the **Record Screen** drop-down button.

3. Select the recording you want to import.

4. Complete the **Insert Slides** dialog box as before.

 Insert the Recording Into Your Project, p. 189

From the **Record Slides** drop-down menu, you can also delete any recordings that you don't want to keep.

Reuse a Recording Elsewhere

You can reuse a recording from one project in another project, or you can export it to reuse somewhere else completely. Exported recordings are saved in **.mp4** format.

To import a recording into another Storyline project:

1. Open the project where you want to import the recording.
2. Go to the **Home** tab.
3. Click the **New Slide** button.
4. Click the **Import** tab.
5. Select **Storyline**.
6. Find and select the project with the recording.
7. Click the **Open** button.
8. Select the slides you want to import.
9. Click the **Import** button.

To import a recording, you can import a video slide, import all the slides in a slide-by-slide recording, or just import one of the slides from a slide-by-slide recording. When you do any of these, the entire recording becomes available from the **Screen Recording** drop-down menu of the new project.

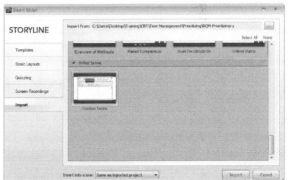

To export a recording:

1. In the project with the recording, go to the **Insert** tab in a page view or the **Home** tab in **Story View**.
2. Click the **Record Screen** drop-down arrow.
3. Select the recording you want to export.
4. In the **Insert Slides** dialog box, right-click the video.
5. Select **Export** movie.
6. Navigate to where you want to save the movie.
7. Enter a name for the movie.
8. Click the **Save** button.
9. Click **OK** in the confirmation dialog box.
10. Cancel out of the **Insert Slides** dialog box.

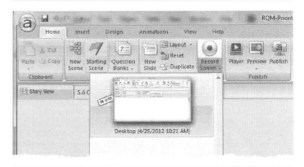

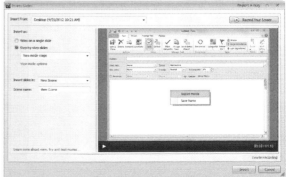

BRIGHT IDEA

In addition to exporting the entire recording, you can also export individual frames. When you right-click the preview as described above, select **Save Frame**. This saves whatever frame is showing at the time as a **.png** graphic.

Notes

The Player

Introduction

The player is a customizable "wrapper" that contains your course and offers useful navigational, branding, and functional features. In addition to the provided features of a menu, resources, glossary, and slide notes, you can also add your own features to the top of the player, such as a link to a lightbox slide to serve as a help page.

In this lesson, you'll learn how to customize the features, visual appearance, and logic behind the player.

In This Chapter

- Player Overview
- Features
- Menu
- Resources
- Glossary
- Colors & Effects
- Text Labels
- Other Settings
- Player File Management

Notes

Getting to Know the Player

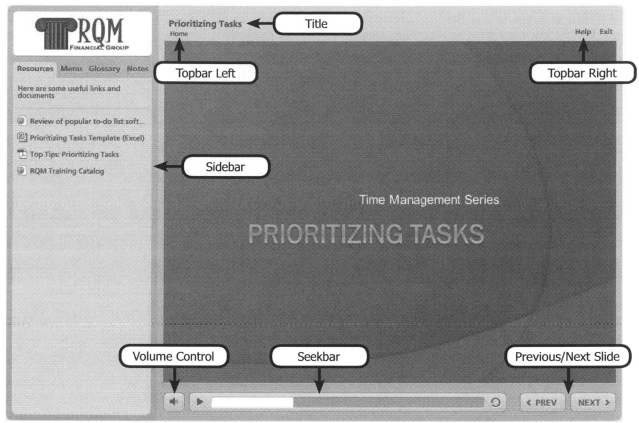

These features can be configured in the **Player Properties** dialog box (with the exception of **Prev** and **Next**). Many of these items can be overridden at the slide level in **Slide Properties**.

Slide Properties, p. 37
Notes, p. 35

- **Resources**: Here you can create a list of useful links to either documents or web pages.
- **Menu**: The menu lists the slides in the course. If you enable navigation, the slide titles become hyperlinks to their respective slides.
- **Glossary**: Use this feature to create a glossary of terms that is available throughout the entire course.
- **Notes**: Whatever you put in the **Notes** tab on your slides appears here in the **Notes** pane.
- **Left/Right Toolbars**: You can add your own custom features to the top right (shown) and/or top left (not shown) of the player. Name the toolbar item and set up the action yourself for custom features.
- **Bottom Controls**: Depending upon how much control you want to give the student, you can enable the volume control and seekbar.

Edit the Player

1. Go to the **Home** tab.
2. Click the **Player** button.
3. Make your changes.
4. Click the **OK** button.

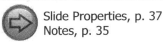

Player Features

Click the **Features** button to turn player features on and off and to indicate where you want them.

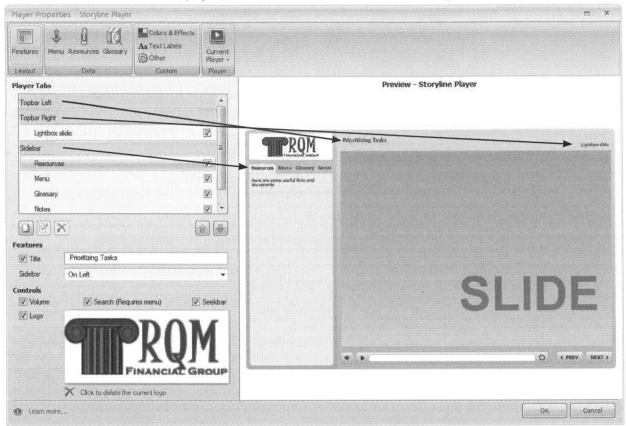

Player Tabs

Use this section to enable, disable, and move the features that appear at the top and the side of the player.

To turn features on and off:

1. Check or uncheck the box next to that feature.

To add a custom feature:

1. Click the **Add** button.
2. In the **Trigger Wizard**, enter the name as you want it to appear in the player.
3. In the **Align** field, indicate if you want it on the right or the left.
4. Set up your action as you normally would.
5. Click the **OK** button.

Available actions:

- Change state of
- Jump to slide
- Jump to Scene
- Lightbox slide
- Close lightbox
- Exit Course
- Jump to URL/File
- Send email to
- Execute JavaScript

 BRIGHT IDEA

You can override some player settings on individual slides.

 Slide Properties, p. 37

 Actions, ch. 10

Player Features (cont'd)

Features that you add yourself can be edited or deleted completely. For example, you can rename the features or change the actions. The pre-existing features (**Resources**, **Menu**, and **Glossary**) can be modified using their respective menu buttons.

To edit a custom player feature:

1. Select the feature in the list.
2. Click the **Edit** button.
3. Make your changes.
4. Click the **OK** button.

To delete a custom player feature:

1. Select the feature in the list.
2. Click the **Delete** button.

To move features to a different part of the player:

1. Select the feature in the list.
2. Click the up and down arrows

Features

Title: Check this box to display the title in the top left corner. The title defaults to the name of your **.story** file. Use the text field to change the displayed title.

Sidebar: Use this menu to put the sidebar on the left or the right side of the player.

Controls

Check or uncheck these boxes to turn these features on or off.

Volume: This puts a convenient volume control button at the bottom of the player. If you do not include this button, students can still control volume by using the settings on their computers or speakers. Be sure to turn this feature off if you don't have audio in the course as it may cause confusion for your students.

Search: If you have the menu enabled, check this box to include a search field at the bottom of the menu panel. This lets the students search on-screen text, slide notes, and question feedback. It does not search alt text.

Seekbar: This puts a progress bar at the bottom of the slide that lets the student see the progress, play and pause the slide, jump to a certain point, and restart the slide.

Logo: If you want to include a logo on top of the sidebar, check this box, and then click the corresponding link to choose your logo file. The following file types are accepted: **.emf**, **.wmf**, **.jpg**, **.jpeg**, **.jfif**, **.jpe**, **.png**, **.bmp**, **.gif**, **.gfa**, **.tif**, and **.tiff**.

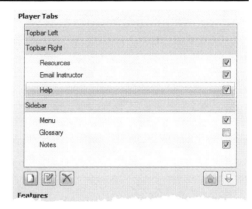

Volume control and seekbar

Menu with search enabled

Menu Options

Click the **Menu** button to customize the **Menu** panel.

The menu is automatically generated with all your slides, based on the story structure. The scenes and slides are ordered based on the numbering in **Story View**.

New Heading

Click this button to add informational headings. For example, if you want to make a sub-heading but don't want to use the first slide in that section for the heading. When the student clicks these informational headings, they are taken to the first slide after the heading.

Insert From Project

If you previously deleted a slide from the menu (see below), you can add it back again by clicking this button and then selecting the slide from the list that appears.

Delete Heading

Use this button to remove the selected slide from the menu. For example, you might not want lightboxed slides to appear in the menu. Deleting the headings here in the menu does not affect how the pages work in the published course.

Move Up/Move Down

Use these buttons to change the order of selected slides. Changing the order in the menu does NOT change the order in which the slides play in the published course. Use this feature to move headings or to rearrange slides in the menu when you have a non-linear course that doesn't follow the standard slide order.

Demote/Promote

Use these buttons to create a hierarchical outline. By default, the first slide of every scene becomes a first-level item, and the other slides in that scene become second-level items. Use the **Demote** button to make a slide a lower-level item and the **Promote** button to make a slide a higher-level item.

Additional Options

Click this button to see additional menu options, detailed on the next page.

Reset From Story

If you've made modifications to the outline that you don't want to keep, click this button to reset the outline to use the naming, ordering, and hierarchy settings of the story pages.

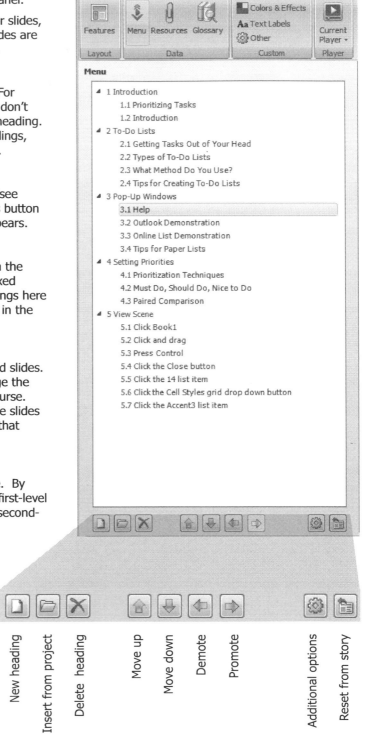

Menu Options (cont'd)

When you click the **Additional Options** button, you get a dialog box with more choices.

Navigation Restriction

This menu determines how the student can navigate through the course using the menu. These settings do not affect the use of the **Next** and **Prev** buttons on the player or any navigational buttons you add to the slides yourself.

- **Free**: The students can view the slides in any order, jumping around freely in the menu.
- **Restricted**: The students can only view the current and previous slides. Students cannot jump ahead.
- **Locked**: Students cannot use the menu to move from slide to slide—it is for informational purposes only.

Wrap Long Menu Titles

If the slide title is too long to fit on a single line in the menu, you can check this box to have it wrap to a second line. If you keep the box unchecked, the end of the title will be cut off.

Show Tooltip on Hover

If you have titles that are cut off because they are too long, and you did not select the wrap option, you can check this box so that the student can hover over the menu item to see a small pop-up box with the full title.

Auto-Collapse Menu as Learner Progresses

For projects with a multi-level menu, check this box if you want levels to collapse (only the "parent" heading shows, not the "child" slides). This is useful in a long course because the students are less likely to have to scroll down to see where they are in the course.

Number Entries in the Menu Automatically

By default, the entries in the menu use the same numbering as the slides in **Story View**. However, if you rearrange slides or delete slides from the menu, the numbering will be out of order. Check this box if you'd like the menu to be numbered in order based on how the slides appear in the menu, not in the story structure.

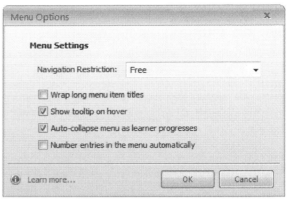

 DESIGN TIP

Free navigation is best when:

- You are building and reviewing the course and want to be able to jump around quickly. (You can turn it off for final publish later, if needed.)
- You want the students to choose what information they want to learn.
- It isn't critical that the students complete everything in the course.
- It doesn't matter in what order the student views the slides.

Restricted navigation is best when:

- It is critical that the students view all the content, such as with new hire orientation or compliance courses.
- You want the students to be able to go back to information they might be unclear about.
- You want to use the course for ongoing reference that the students can re-visit at any time.

Locked navigation is best when:

- It is critical that the students view all the content, such as with new hire orientation or compliance courses.
- You do not expect the students to go back into the course later for reference.

Setting Up Resources

Click the **Resources** button to add or edit items on the **Resources** list.

To change the description at the top of the list:

1. Type your text in the **Description** field.

To add a web link resource:

1. Click the **Add** button.
2. In the **Title** field, type the name of the resource as you want it to appear in the **Resources** list.
3. Select **URL**.
4. Type the web address you want to link to.
5. Click the **Save** button.

To add a file resource:

1. Click the **Add** button.
2. In the **Title** field, type the name of the resource as you want it to appear in the **Resources** list.
3. Select **File**.
4. Click the **Browse** button.
5. Find and select the file you want to use.
6. Click the **Open** button.
7. Click the **Save** button.

To edit a resource:

1. Select the entry.
2. Click the **Edit** button.
3. Make your changes.
4. Click the **Save** button.

To delete a resource:

1. Select the resource.
2. Click the **Delete** button.

To change the order of the resources:

1. Select the item you want to move.
2. Click the **Move up** or **Move down** buttons.

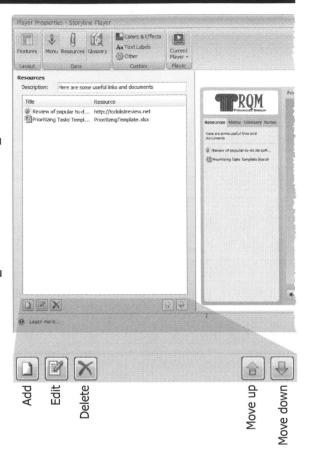

Add   Edit   Delete   Move up   Move down

Link to a website

Link to a file

Setting Up the Glossary

Click the **Glossary** button to add or edit items in the glossary. Entries are arranged in alphabetical order, regardless of the order in which you enter them.

To add a glossary entry:

1. Click the **Add** button.
2. In the **Term** field, type the item to be defined.
3. In the **Definition** field, type the definition.
4. Click the **Save** button.

To edit an entry:

1. Select the entry.
2. Click the **Edit** button.
3. Make your changes.
4. Click the **Save** button.

To delete an entry:

1. Select the entry.
2. Click the **Delete** button.

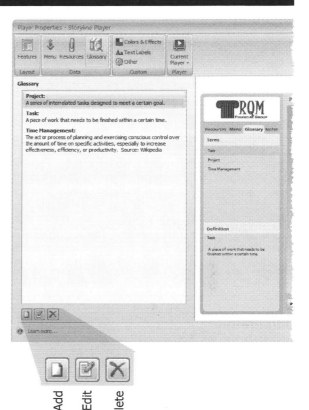

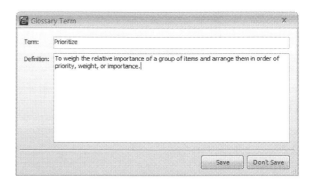

Change Colors & Effects

Click the **Colors & Effects** button to change the colors and font for the player.

Color Schemes

The color scheme governs the colors used for the individual player elements such as background fills, text, hover colors, etc. You can select from a pre-made list of color schemes, or create your own.

To apply a pre-made color scheme:

1. Click the **Color Scheme** drop-down menu.
2. Select the color scheme you want.

To edit a color scheme:

1. Click the **Color scheme** drop-down menu.
2. Select the color scheme most similar to what you want.
3. Click the **Show advanced color editing** link. **(A)**
4. Click the **Edit item** drop-down list. **(B)**
5. Select the item type you want to modify. **(C)**
6. Select the item's feature you want to modify. **(D)**
7. Click either of the color drop-down menus. **(E)**
8. Select the color you want.
9. In the **Transparency** field, change the number if you want the feature to be partially (between 0 and 100) or fully (100) transparent.
10. Repeat the process from step 4 to change additional items and features.

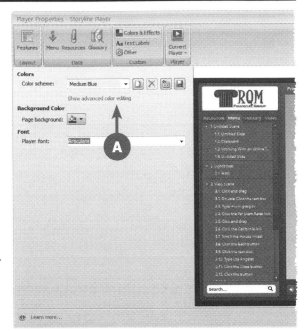

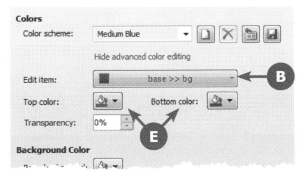

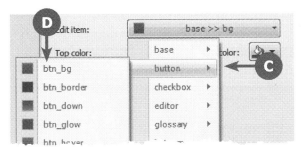

Change Colors & Effects (cont'd)

To duplicate an existing color scheme (so you can modify it without changing the original)**:**

1. Select the color scheme from the drop-down menu.
2. Click the **Duplicate the selected color scheme** button.

To delete a saved color scheme:

1. Select the color scheme from the drop-down menu.
2. Click the **Delete the selected color scheme** button.

To restore a color scheme to its previously saved settings:

1. Select the color scheme from the drop-down menu.
2. Click the **Reset the color scheme** button.

To save a modified color scheme:

1. Click the **Save the selected color theme to a file** button.
2. Enter a name for the theme.
3. Click the **OK** button.

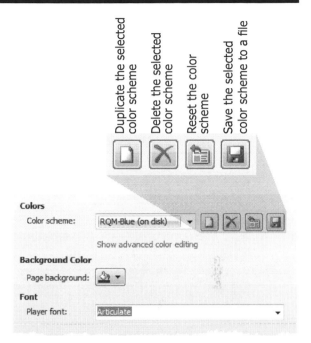

Change Text Labels

Text labels are system-generated messages that may appear throughout the published course. For example, students might get a message telling them they must answer a quiz question before continuing.

Click the **Text Labels** button to change the text for any of these system-generated labels.

To change the language used for the labels:

1. Click the **Language** drop-down menu.
2. Select the language you want.

To customize individual labels:

1. Find the row for the text you want to change.
2. Edit the text in the **Custom Text** column.

If you are customizing the labels for just the project you are in, you don't have to do anything else. However, if you are likely to need the same customizations in a different project, then you may want to save the file. Text labels are saved as **.xml** files.

To save a set of labels:

1. Click the **Save** button.
2. Find and select the location for the file.
3. Enter a name for the file.
4. Click the **Save** button.

If you saved a label set on your computer, it will be available to you in the **Language** drop-down menu. If you want to use a label set that someone else created and saved, you can load it onto your computer to appear on your drop-down list.

To load a set of labels:

1. Click the **Load** button.
2. Find and select the label file you want to use.
3. Click the **Open** button.

Built-In
English
Chinese Simplified
Chinese Traditional
Dutch
French
German
Italian
Japanese
Korean
Portuguese
Spanish

💡 BRIGHT IDEAS

- Click the **Update preview** button to see your text labels in the preview area on the right.

- If you don't like the changes you've made, you can reset the text labels at any time. Simply re-select the original option from the **Language** drop-down menu. For example, if you select **English** from the menu, the text labels change back to the English defaults.

Other Player Settings

Click the **Other** button to change other player settings.

Browser Settings

Published projects play in a browser (except when using the iPad app).

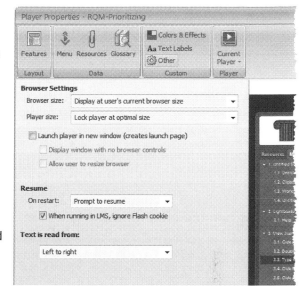

Browser Size

- **Display at user's current browser size**: The window matches the user's current browser size.

- **Resize browser to optimal size**: The browser window appears at the same size as the course.

- **Resize browser to fill screen**: The browser fills the user's screen.

Player Size

- **Scale player to fill browser window**: The published course size matches the browser size (may be smaller or larger than the story size).

- **Lock player at optimal size**: The published course size matches the story size (shows at 100%).

 Story Size, p. 15

Launch Player in New Window

If you check this box, the course opens to a blank page with a **Launch** button, which opens the presentation in a new window. This is most often used if you are not using a learning management system. Selecting this setting gives you two additional options normally governed by the LMS:

- **Display window with no browser controls**: This turns off the student's browser toolbars. This gives more room for the course and prevents the student from using the browser's **Back** button.

- **Allow user to resize browser**: Check this box if you want to give the student control over the browser size.

If you are using an LMS, do a test to make sure this feature doesn't interfere with tracking.

 DESIGN TIP

For highest quality, fill the screen (to avoid a distracting view of the desktop or other applications), and lock the presentation to the optimal size (so images aren't enlarged so much that they become fuzzy).

Resize browser to fill screen & scale presentation to fill browser

Resize browser to fill screen & lock presentation to optimal size

Resize browser to optimal size & lock presentation to optimal size

Other Player Settings (cont'd)

Resume

These options govern what happens when a student exits a course and then comes back to it.

- **Prompt to resume**: Check this option to ask your students if they want to resume where they left off last time or start over at the beginning of the course.

- **Always resume**: Choose this option if the course should resume where the student left off without asking.

- **Never resume**: Choose this option if the course should start over without asking.

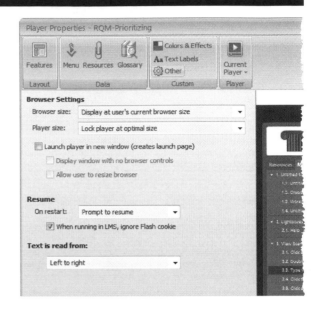

When Running in LMS, Ignore Flash Cookie

The prompt-to-resume feature can be managed by your learning management system (if your LMS supports that feature) or by Flash "cookies" stored on the user's computer. If you uncheck this box, the course (when in an LMS) will first use the data from the LMS to resume the course where the user left off. If you are not using an LMS or if the LMS does not support the resume feature, the course will resume based on the Flash cookie.

Text Is Read From

Change this setting from **Left to right** to **Right to left** if you are using a language that reads right to left.

Managing Player Files

Use the **Current Player** drop-down button to manage your player files, such as opening, saving, importing, exporting, resetting, and deleting.

To open a different player file:
1. Click the **Current Player** button.
2. Select **Open**.
3. Select the player you want to use.

To save the current player file:
1. Click the **Current Player** button.
2. Select **Save**.

To save the current player file under a different name:
1. Click the **Current Player** button.
2. Select **Save as**.
3. Enter a new name.
4. Click the **OK** button.

To import a player file:
1. Click the **Current Player** button.
2. Select **Import**.
3. Find and select the file you want to import.
4. Click the **Open** button.

To export a player file:
1. Click the **Current Player** button.
2. Select **Export**.
3. Find and select the location where you want to save the file.
4. Enter a name for the file.
5. Click the **Save** button.

To reset a player to its previously saved settings:
1. Click the **Current Player** button.
2. Select **Reset**.

To delete the currently open player file:
1. Click the **Current Player** button.
2. Click the **Delete** button.
3. Click **Yes**.

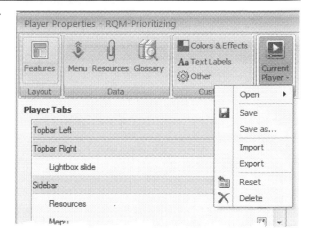

💡 BRIGHT IDEA

Use **Open** if the file is already saved on your computer. Use **Import** if the file is saved somewhere else.

Use the **Export** option when you want to share the files with someone else who can then import the file.

Notes

Publishing

Introduction

As you create and edit your Articulate course, you are working in a Storyline (**.story**) file. While this file is necessary for you to create and edit your course, it is not the file that students use to view the course.

When you are ready to share your course, it needs to be published to the appropriate format, based on how you plan to distribute the course. When you do this, a new set of files is created. These published files are what you would burn to a CD, post to the web, copy to a shared network drive, or load to a learning management system (LMS).

In this chapter, you'll learn how to publish your course to the following formats:

- Web
- Articulate Online
- Learning Management System (SCORM/AICC)
- CD
- Word

Plus, you'll learn special tips for publishing to mobile devices using HTML5 or the Articulate Mobile Player app for the iPad.

In This Chapter

- Publishing Formats
- Publishing Process
- Mobile Publishing
- Publish to Web
- Publish to Articulate Online
- Publish to LMS
- Publish to CD
- Publish to Word

Notes

Publishing Formats

Web

The **Web** option is used when you want to post files to an internet or intranet site, but don't need it to track users' progress. This is also a good method for reviewing the courses yourself on your own computer or as part of a formal review cycle, since the files can be uploaded to any web server or posted on a shared drive. You can also use this option for posting content to be viewed on mobile devices.

Articulate Online

Articulate Online, Articulate's hosted online tracking and delivery system, lets you track how students interact with your e-learning courses and assessments.

LMS (Learning Management System)

If you will post your courses on a learning management system, use this option. Then, select from the following publishing standards that govern how your course (the content) and the LMS (the host) communicate with each other. Your LMS provider should be able to tell you which option you need to use.

- **SCORM 1.2**: SCORM stands for Sharable Content Object Reference Model and is the most commonly used e-learning standard for how courses and LMSs communicate with each other. SCORM 1.2 is an older version of the standard but is still supported by most LMSs today.

- **SCORM 2004**: This is the most current version of SCORM.

- **AICC:** This publication standard was developed by the Aviation Industry CBT (Computer-Based Training) Committee (AICC). While not as prevalent as SCORM, its specifications are broadly accepted among LMS providers servicing both aviation and non-aviation users.

You can also publish to the LMS format if your courses will be viewed on a mobile device.

CD

Use this option to create files you can burn to a CD that automatically plays when put into a computer. This is useful for users who may not have access to the internet, and you do not need to track progress. File sizes for this method are larger because all images are published at highest quality.

Word

You can publish to Word to help with review cycles or to use as a handout. This is an excellent way to share the content with teammates for feedback or collaboration.

 BRIGHT IDEA

You can publish for mobile devices using any of the formats except Word.

Publish a Course

The high-level process for publishing the course is the same no matter what format you use. The high-level steps are listed below, with details about the different publishing formats on the following pages.

To publish a course:

1. Go to the **Home** tab in **Story View** or **Slide View**.
2. Click the **Publish** button.
3. Click the tab on the left side to select a publish format.
4. In the **Title** field, enter the course title.
5. In the **Title** field, click the **Browse** button. **(A)**
6. Enter project information. (See next page.)
7. Click the **OK** button.
8. In the **Folder** field, click the **Browse** button. **(B)**
9. Navigate to the folder where you want to save the published course.
10. Click **Open**.
11. Select the options you want for mobile publishing, if applicable. **(C)**
12. Click the link in the **Quality** field. **(D)**
13. Enter the quality settings you want. (See page 224.)
14. Enter any additional publishing information for the format you chose. (See pages 227–231.)
15. Click the **Publish** button.

CAUTION

- Always publish to your local drive (your computer) instead of to a network or USB drive. You can move the files after you've published them.

- Some web servers and LMSs have strict rules about file names. When you name your published files in the **Title** field, it's best to avoid special characters. In some cases, you may even need to avoid spaces.

BRIGHT IDEA

If you want to check or change your player settings, you can do it right from the **Publish** dialog box. Simply click the link in the **Publish** field to open the **Player Properties** dialog box and make whatever changes you want.

 Player, ch. 14

Project Information

You can enter optional project information for any project, regardless of publishing format, by clicking the **Browse** button in the **Title** field of the **Publish** dialog box. This information can be used by your learning management system, the Articulate Mobile Player app, and possibly other platforms that pull information about your project.

- **Title**: This field is tied to the **Title** field in the **Publish** dialog box. Changes to one are reflected in the other.

- **Use**: If your delivery platform (such as the iPad app) accepts a thumbnail image of the course, it is pulled from this field. By default, the thumbnail of the first slide is used. If you'd like to use the thumbnail of a different slide, click the link under the thumbnail, and select another slide from the project.

- **Description**: This field is tied to the **Title** field in the **Publish** dialog box. Changes to one are reflected in the other.

- **Keywords**: Enter keywords, separated by commas, that relate to your content to help students find your course.

- **Author**: Enter the author of the course, which can be a person, company, department, etc.

- **Email/Website**: Enter contact information in the form of an email address and website.

- **Duration**: Providing students with the duration of the course can help set expectations and help them plan their time. You have two choices:
  - **Calculate automatically**: With this method, Storyline creates an estimate based on slide and layer length.
  - **Manual**: If you select this option from the drop-down menu, you can enter your own length description in the field provided.

- **Date**: You have two choices for the date of publication:
  - **Last published**: With this option, Storyline uses the date of the publish.
  - **Custom**: You can enter your own date, by either typing it in or using the calendar icon to select a date.

- **Version**: To help you manage multiple versions of the published course, you can enter a version number here.

- **Identifier**: A unique code is generated for the course, useful when publishing to an LMS.

Quality Settings

When you publish your course, all of the data is compressed, resulting in faster download times. While compression makes your files smaller, it can also cause your course to lose image and audio quality—the higher the compression the lower the quality and vice-versa.

When you click the link in the **Quality** field in the **Publish** dialog box, you can control the compression settings for your course so you can find the best balance between compression and quality.

You can use the standard option or customize the quality settings for video, audio, and images individually.

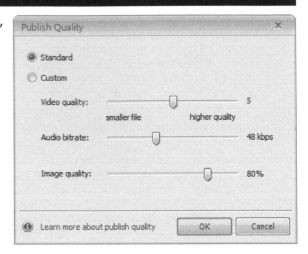

Standard

By default, Storyline projects are set to **Standard**, which is an optimized compression level designed to keep file size low and still maintain quality.

Custom

Select **Custom** if you'd like to manually set the quality settings for the different media types.

Video Quality

Move the slider to the left on the 9-point scale for a smaller file (meaning a higher compression level and possibly lower quality) or to the right for higher quality (meaning lower compression and a higher file size).

Audio Bitrate

Use the slider to select an audio bitrate between 16 kbps and 160 kbps. The higher the bitrate, the higher the quality and the larger the file size.

Image Quality

Just as with video, move the slider to the left for a smaller file (meaning higher compression and lower quality) or to the right for higher quality (with lower compression and bigger file size).

 POWER TIP

What is bitrate?

The bitrate determines how many points along the sound wave curve are captured in a digital file. It is measured in kbps (kilobits per second). The more points captured, the higher the quality and the higher the file size.

Lower bitrate   Higher bitrate

 BRIGHT IDEA

If file size is a concern, create a test course with a few pages of representative media. Start with the lowest possible settings, publish it, and test the quality of the output. Go up a level on any of the settings if you aren't happy with the audio. Continue until you reach an acceptable level of quality.

Mobile Publishing

The **Web**, **Articulate Online**, **LMS**, and **CD** formats have three options for mobile publishing.

If you check any of these boxes when you publish, the course still publishes the "traditional" way, and extra files are included that work on mobile devices.

Include HTML5 Output

Check this box if you want your course to output in an HTML5 format. This format does not require the Flash player, so it is appropriate for non-Flash devices such as the iPhone and iPad.

Use Articulate Mobile Player on iPad

The Articulate Mobile Player is a free iPad (not iPhone) app available in iTunes. If a student opens the link to your course on an iPad with this app, the course opens in the app instead of in a browser.

Allow Downloading for Offline Viewing

The iPad app lets students download the content to the app's library, letting them view the content offline. Uncheck this box if you don't want the student to download the project to the app, but only view it when online.

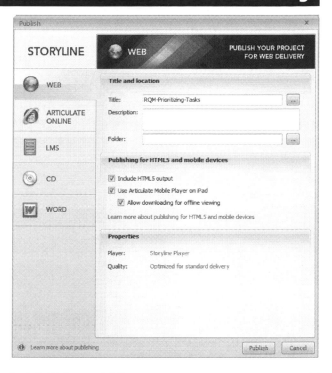

 DESIGN TIPS

How do you decide which options to use?

- HTML5 can be interpreted differently by different browsers and devices, so if publishing to this format, be sure to test it in HTML5 to make sure it works properly.

- The iPad app allows the course to function as closely as possible to your intended design, versus viewing the content on an iPad via a browser.

- The iPad app cannot interface with an LMS and cannot access password-protected content (at the time of this book's publish).

- If you *import* Flash content into your project (such as an Engage interaction), it will not be converted to HTML, and will not play in an HTML5-only (non-Flash) platform.

- If you include HTML5 and iPad app outputs, the course checks for the iPad app and plays that format. Next it looks for the Flash player and plays in that format. If neither is available, it looks for HTML5 compatibility and plays in that format. If none of these options are available, a message is displayed to the student with instructions.

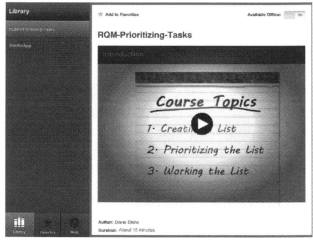

The Articulate Mobile Player App

 BRIGHT IDEA

The world of mobile devices and HTML5 changes quickly. Be sure to refer to the latest guidance from Articulate on best practices and options for publishing to mobile devices.

Post-Publish Options

After publishing, you get a **Publish Successful** dialog box with several time-saving options:

- **View Project**: Click this button to view the project in a web browser. This is a great way to preview your course and to make sure everything works.

- **Email**: This generates an email with a **.zip** file of the course and instructions as attachments. This is a great way to share the course with reviewers (as long as the course is not too large to send in an email).

- **FTP**: Using the File Transfer Protocol (FTP), you can upload the published files from your computer to a server (such as a website or LMS site). You will need FTP account details, such as username, password, etc.

- **ZIP**: This zips your published files, making it easy to share, archive, or post them to an LMS. Many LMSs require a **.zip** format.

- **Open Folder**: Use this option to view the folder that contains the published files.

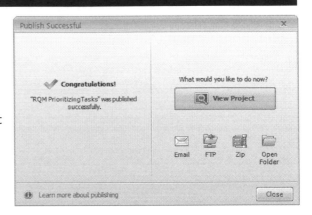

Published Files

The published output for the **Web** option produces the files as shown to the right.

- **story.html**: This is the file you would double-click to run the course off of your computer or a server. When posting the files to the web, this is the file to link to in order to launch the course.

- **story_content**: This folder contains all the media assets for the course, such as audio, video, animation, and image files.

- **external_files**: If you use the **Jump to URL/File** action to launch a document, that document is stored in this file.

- **WebObjects**: If you included a web object from a file, those files are stored here.

If you include the HTML5 and/or iPad app options, you still link to the **story.html** file. Logic in that file launches the appropriate HTML5 or iOS files, if appropriate.

If you are publishing to Articulate Online or an LMS, there are extra files that contain the logic for "talking" to the LMS.

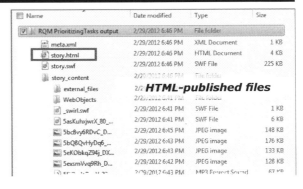

HTML-published files

HTML-published files with HTML5 and iPad app enabled

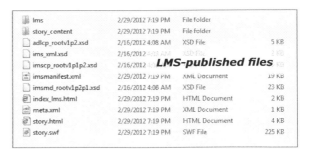

LMS-published files

 CAUTION

- If you rearrange or rename any of the files, the course may not run properly.

- When you post your files (to a web server, the LMS, etc.), be sure to include ALL of the published files.

Publish to Web

Publishing to **Web** is very straightforward. There are no additional settings specific to web publishing over those already discussed in this chapter.

Publish to Articulate Online

When you publish to Articulate Online (AO), Storyline uploads the course to the AO-hosted online tracking and delivery system. Publishing to this format includes the following additional fields.

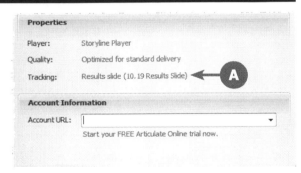

Tracking

Click the link in the **Tracking** field **(A)** to configure when and how completion status is reported.

Reporting

- **Report status to AO as**: AO accepts four different options for completion status:
  - Passed/Incomplete
  - Passed/Failed
  - Completed/Incomplete
  - Completed/Failed

- **Communicate resume data**: Resume data includes answers to questions, values for variables, and the page where the student left off. The course passes this information to Articulate Online to be stored until the student launches the course again. Indicate if you want that resume data to be sent when the course is complete or after every slide. **After Every Slide** is a good option in situations where you think the student might have internet connection disruptions.

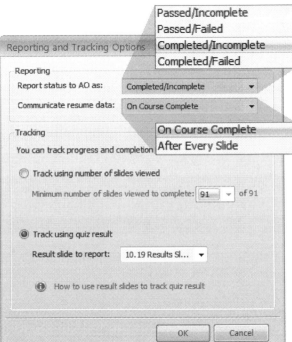

Tracking

- **Track using number of slides viewed**: Use this method if you want to track completion based on whether the student visited all (or a certain number) of the pages. In the drop-down menu, choose the minimum number of slides the student must view to earn completion status.

- **Track using quiz result**: Use this option if you want to track the student based on the status of one of your results slides. Select the option, and then select which results slide to use.

Account URL

Enter the web address for your Articulate Online account to post the course to the Articulate Online servers.

 CAUTION

Be careful about requiring all the pages to be viewed if some of your pages are optional, such as a branching scenario or lightboxed slides.

Publish to LMS

If you will host your content on a SCORM- or AICC-compliant LMS, use the **LMS** tab when publishing. In addition to the standard publishing settings, select which LMS standard to use and the reporting and tracking requirements.

LMS

Select **SCORM 1.2**, **SCORM 2004**, or **AICC** from the drop-down menu. If you select **SCORM 2004**, further select the 2nd, 3rd, or 4th edition. Your LMS provider should be able to tell you which of the standards is best for that LMS.

Reporting and Tracking

The **Tracking** link and the **Reporting and Tracking** button both take you to the same dialog box.

Reporting tab

- **LMS**: This field is the same as the LMS field on the previous screen.

- **LMS Course Information**: This information is the same as the data in the **Project Information** dialog box. Enter the information as you'd like it to appear in the LMS catalog.

- **LMS Lesson SCORM Information**: Enter the title for the lesson.

- **Identifier**: Enter a unique identifier for the course. Your LMS may have specific guidelines about what this should be.

- **Report status to LMS as**: Storyline can send one of four different options for completion status:
  - Passed/Incomplete
  - Passed/Failed
  - Completed/Incomplete
  - Completed/Failed

- **Creator**: For AICC only, the creator is pulled from the **Author** field in the **Project Information** dialog box.

- **Filename(URL)**: For AICC only, enter the location where the course will be hosted on your LMS.

Tracking tab

- **Track using number of slides viewed**: Use this method if you want to track completion based on whether the student visited all (or a certain number) of the pages. In the drop-down menu, choose the minimum number of slides the student must view to earn completion status.

- **Track using quiz result**: Use this option if you want track the student based on the status of one of your results slides. Select the option, and then select which results slide to use.

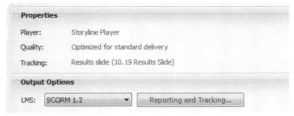

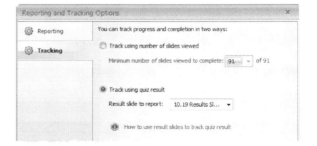

 DESIGN TIP

How do you decide which reporting status to send? It may be an instructional design decision (for example, **completed** if based on slide views and **passed** if based on quiz results). However, some LMSs require a certain setting and will not accept any of the others. Be sure to check with your LMS for details or conduct an early test to see what works.

Publish to CD

The **CD** option has the exact same choices as the **Web** option.

When you publish to CD, Storyline automatically creates an autorun file. When your students insert the CD into their computers, the course automatically starts.

Copy all of the published output files to the CD.

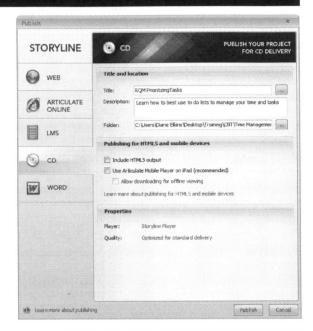

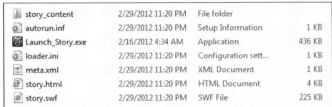

Use the Word option to convert your story to help with the review process or to create related documentation such as reference manuals, job aids, etc.

Indicate if you want to include layers and/or notes and how big you want the thumbnail image of each slide to be.

Notes

Appendix A

Notes

Useful Shortcuts

Feature	Shortcut
Managing Objects	
Select all	Ctrl + A
Cut	Ctrl + X
Copy	Ctrl + C
Paste	Ctrl + V
Duplicate	Ctrl + D
Undo	Ctrl + Z
Redo	Ctrl + Y
Group objects	Ctrl + G
Ungroup objects	Shift + Ctrl + G
Add trigger	Ctrl + K
Open Format Shape dialog box	Ctrl + Enter
Open Size and Position dialog box	Ctrl + Shift + Enter
Show/Hide guidelines	Shift + F9
Move object by 1 pixel	Ctrl + arrow key
Enlarge/Reduce object size by 1 pixel	Shift + Ctrl + arrow
Text Editing	
Bold	Ctrl + B
Italics	Ctrl + I
Underline	Ctrl + U
Subscript	Ctrl + =
Superscript	Shift + Ctrl + =
Grow font	Ctrl + >
Shrink font	Ctrl + <
Align left	Ctrl + L
Align center	Ctrl + E
Align right	Ctrl + R
Spell check	F7
Find	Ctrl + F
Insert hyperlink	Ctrl + K
Select text in object when the object is selected	F2

Feature	Shortcut
File Management	
Save	Ctrl + S
New project	Ctrl + N
Open project	Ctrl + O
Insert	
Insert picture	Ctrl + J
Insert text box	Ctrl + T
Insert new slide	Ctrl + M
View	
Normal view	F3
Slide master	F4
Feedback master	F5
Close slide tab	Ctrl + W
Preview/Publish	
Preview all	F12
Preview scene	Shift + F12
Preview slide	Ctrl + F12
Publish	F10
Edit current slide (in Preview mode)	F2
While Playing Timeline	
Toggle play/pause	Spacebar
Insert cuepoint	c
During Screen Recording	
Stop recording	Esc
Pause/Resume	Alt + D
Take screenshot	PrintScreen

Main Ribbons and File Menu

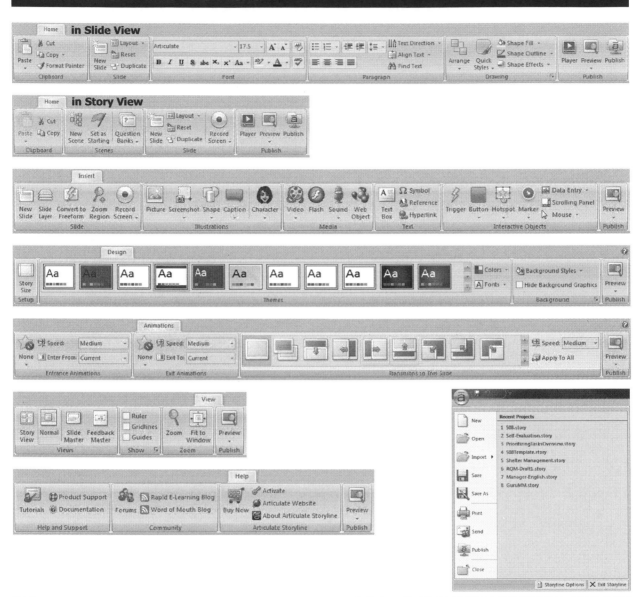

Context-Sensitive Ribbons

Picture Tools

Drawing Tools

Context-Sensitive Ribbons (cont'd.)

Character: Design Tools

Character: Format Tools

Movie Tools   Sound Tools

Web Object Tools

Button Tools

Radio Button Tools

Check Box Tools

Marker Tools

Mouse Tools

Button and Marker Icon Options

Button Icons

Marker Icons

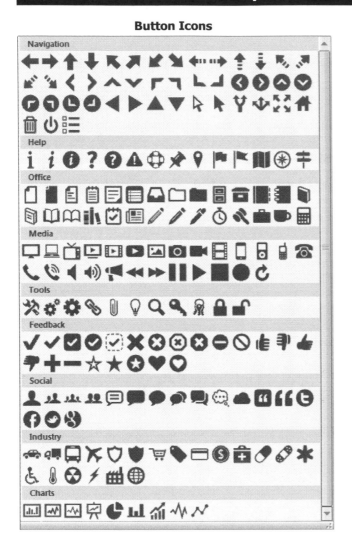

File Extension Guide

Extension	Description
Storyline-Generated Files	
.story	Storyline project file
.storytemplate	Storyline template file
.anthm	Storyline theme
Articulate Studio Files	
.quiz	Articulate Quizmaker file
.intr	Articulate Engage file
Accepted Image Types	
.bmp	Windows bitmap
.emf	Windows enhanced metafile
.gfa	Graphics interchange format
.gif	
.jfif	JPEG file interchange format
.jpe	
.jpeg	
.jpg	
.png	Portable network graphics
.tif	Tag image file format
.tiff	
.wmf	Windows metafile
Accepted Mouse Cursor Types	
.ani	Windows animated cursor
.cur	Windows cursor

Extension	Description
Accepted Audio Types	
.aac	Advanced audio coding file
.aif	Audio interchange file format
.aiff	
.m4a	Apple lossless audio file
.mp3	Common compressed audio format
.ogg	Ogg Vorbis compressed audio file
.wav	Windows audio file
.wma	Windows Media audio file
Accepted Video Types	
.3g2	3G video files
.3gp	
.asf	Windows Media file
.avi	Microsoft video format
.dv	Digital video file
.flv	Flash video
.m1v	MPEG-1 and MPEG-2 movie files
.m2v	
.mov	QuickTime file
.mpe	MPEG movie file
.mpeg	
.mpg	
.qt	QuickTime file
.swf	Shockwave Flash file (also an accepted animation type)
.wmv	Windows Media file

Change Storyline Options

To change the Storyline options:

1. Click the **File** button.
2. Click the **Storyline Options** button.
3. Make the changes you want.
4. Click **OK**.

Storyline Options

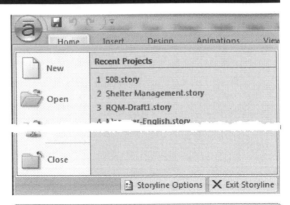

Check for Updates at Startup

Keep this box checked if you want Storyline to check for any updates to the software every time you start Storyline. Uncheck the box if you do not want to check for updates automatically. You can still check for updates any time from the **Help** tab.

Enable Publishing for Manual Upload to Articulate Online

Articulate Online is a learning management system made by Articulate. Use this option if you aren't connected to the internet, but still want to publish to upload later.

Reset "Don't Show Again" Prompts

Throughout the software, there are warning messages, such as "Are you sure you want to delete this slide?". Those dialog boxes have a check box that you can check if you want to turn off that particular type of warning message. Click this button if you want to turn all of the warning message types back on.

Spelling Options

Click this button to change the settings for the spell check feature. For example, you can choose to ignore capitalized words, select a language for the dictionary, or load a custom dictionary.

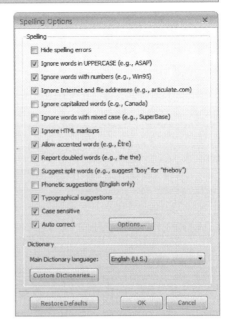

Change Storyline Options (cont'd)

AutoCorrect Options

AutoCorrect fixes common spelling mistakes as you type. For example, if you type "teh," AutoCorrect will change it to "the." Click this button to change the settings. For example, you can turn AutoCorrect off or add your own autocorrections.

 TIME SAVER

AutoCorrect can be used for more than just typos! You can also use it to automate text you type frequently. For example, you can add an entry that changes "sata" to "Select all that apply."

Proxy Settings

The proxy settings are only for publishing to Articulate Online. A proxy server is an intermediary server between your computer and the Internet. It serves as an added security feature.

Use Internet Explorer Proxy Settings: If you select this radio button, you can publish to Articulate Online using your Internet Explorer proxy settings.

Use Proxy Server: If you select this radio button, you can enter specific proxy settings. This may be necessary if your company uses a proxy server and you are publishing to Articulate Online.

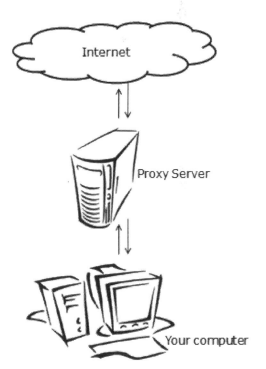

Accessibility

Accessibility in e-learning refers to making courses compatible with various assistive technology devices used by people with disabilities. There are three main classes of disability that affect e-learning: visual, auditory, and motor.

Impairment	Common Assistive Devices	Considerations for E-Learning
Visual Low vision No vision Color blindness	Screen readers that read information about what is happening on-screen to the user. Refreshable braille displays that create dynamic braille descriptions of what is happening on screen. Screen magnifiers that enlarge all or part of what is happening on screen.	In order for screen readers and braille displays to describe what is happening on screen, they need to be "told." Therefore, you'll need to add descriptive text, known as "alt text", to course elements for these assistive devices to read. Be sure that there are no elements that require recognition of color. Color can be used, as long as it is not the only way to tell what something means. For example, you can include a green check and a red X to indicate right or wrong, because the check and the X alone can convey the meaning. But a red and green dot would not work, since the student would need to distinguish between the colors to determine meaning. Use strong value contrast (light vs. dark), so those with low vision or color blindness can recognize on-screen elements. For example, a light blue caption on a light background may be hard to read for those with vision challenges. Vision is required in order to use a mouse properly. Visually impaired students generally do not use a mouse, instead relying on keyboard navigation through their screen reader. Therefore, course elements must be keyboard-accessible.
Auditory Hard of hearing Deafness	Closed captioning systems	For individuals with auditory impairments, it is necessary to provide a transcript of any important audio elements in the course. For static content, this can be done with a static transcript text box. For multimedia content timed to audio, the captions should also be timed to audio.
Mobility Limited dexterity No manual skills	Alternate navigation devices such as keyboards, joysticks, trackballs, and even breathing devices	For those with limited mobility, be sure that any interactive element (such as a button) is large enough for someone with rough motor skills to use. Make sure all course elements are keyboard accessible. If a course is keyboard accessible, then it will work with most other mobility-assistive devices.

Another factor to consider is cognitive impairments such as learning disabilities or dyslexia. Courses are more accessible to those with cognitive impairments when there are no time constraints. For example, you can include play/pause/rewind controls and avoid timed elements, such as a timed test.

Accessibility Requirements and Guidelines

There are two main reasons to make your courses accessible:

1. You want your courses to be available to those in your target audience who may have a disability.
2. You may be required by law.

Internationally, the World Wide Web Consortium (W3C) provides web content accessibility guidelines. In addition, many countries have their own standards and requirements. In the United States, Section 508 of the Rehabilitation Act of 1973 (and later amended) requires that information technology (including e-learning) used by the federal government be accessible to those with disabilities. Many other organizations choose to adopt that standard on their own. Go to www.section508.gov for more detailed information on the standards and the requirements.

Creating a 508-Compliant Course

The following pages contain the accessibility standards for web pages from the Section 508 requirements for web-based intranet and internet information and applications, along with the corresponding procedures in Storyline.

This guide is not intended to be a stand-alone guide, but rather to be used in conjunction with other educational resources (such as www.section508.gov) and thorough accessibility testing.

Section 508 - 1194.22

(a) A text equivalent for every non-text element shall be provided (e.g., via "alt", "longdesc", or in element content).

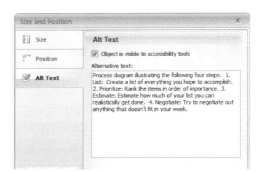

- Add alt text to each non-text object that conveys content. For example, if you have an image of a diagram, you'll need to add a text description of that diagram for screen readers to read.

- Turn off alt text for objects that do not convey content.

- When managing alt text, be sure to remember objects on master slides, objects on layers, and objects imported from templates.

- For static slides, use the **Notes** tab to enter transcript text, and then enable the **Notes** tab in the player.

  Alt Text, p. 68
Slide Notes, p. 35
Player, ch. 14

(b) Equivalent alternatives for any multimedia presentation shall be synchronized with the presentation.

- Add text boxes with captioning timed to audio or video (if applicable). Captions can appear on the main slide or be put on a slide layer that can be turned on and off by the student with a button.

  Timing Objects, p. 66
Slide Layers, p. 106
Show/Hide Layer Actions, p. 122

(c) Web pages shall be designed so that all information conveyed with color is also available without color, for example from context or markup.

- This is primarily done through your own design of the course. Avoid any element in which color is the only way of communicating information. As a test, print out screens in grayscale to determine if the course elements can still be understood.

- Word bank and hotspot questions use only red and green indicators to designate correct/incorrect answers during the post-quiz review. However, these question types are not accessible for other reasons and should not be used in an accessible course.

  Post-Quiz Review, p. 177

(d) Documents shall be organized so they are readable without requiring an associated style sheet.

(e) Redundant text links shall be provided for each active region of a server-side image map.

(f) Client-side image maps shall be provided instead of server-side image maps except where the regions cannot be defined with an available geometric shape.

- Storyline does not use style sheets or image maps, so these standards are not applicable.

Creating a 508-Compliant Course (cont'd)

(g) Row and column headers shall be identified for data tables.

(h) Markup shall be used to associate data cells and header cells for data tables that have two or more logical levels of row or column headers.

- Storyline does not have a tool to create tables. If you create a table elsewhere and bring it in as a graphic, be sure to provide detailed alt text for the content in the table.

(i) Frames shall be titled with text that facilitates frame identification and navigation.

- Storyline does not use frames, so this part of the standard is not applicable for a Storyline project.

(j) Pages shall be designed to avoid causing the screen to flicker with a frequency greater than 2 Hz and lower than 55 Hz.

- Anything that flashes or flickers needs to be either slower than 2 times per second or faster than 55 times per second. Anything in between that range could cause seizures in some people.

- If you incorporate animations, make sure you do not have anything appearing and disappearing at a frequency in this range. Plus, if you import animations, animated gifs, or videos, make sure you work outside of the prohibited range.

(k) A text-only page, with equivalent information or functionality, shall be provided to make a web site comply with the provisions of this part, when compliance cannot be accomplished in any other way. The content of the text-only page shall be updated whenever the primary page changes.

- You can provide text equivalents through alt text, captioning, on-screen text, and the **Notes** panel. If this is not adequate, you can link to a document using the **Jump to URL/File** action. Just be sure that the document in question is also accessible.

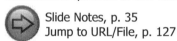

Slide Notes, p. 35
Jump to URL/File, p. 127

(l) When pages utilize scripting languages to display content, or to create interface elements, the information provided by the script shall be identified with functional text that can be read by assistive technology.

- This standard means that in addition to the alt text you set up as part of (a), system controls need to be understandable by screen readers and accessible using keyboard navigation. Most of a published course is accessible by keyboard, but there are a few that aren't, meaning they should not be used in a 508-compliant course.

- In a quiz, only use multiple choice, multiple response, true/false, matching drop-down, sequence drop-down, Likert, fill in the blank, numeric, short answer, and essay question types (and their survey or freeform equivalents). The other types of questions are not accessible.

 Questions & Quizzes, ch. 12

- In addition, objects being read by a screen reader or tabbed to via keyboard navigation should come in a logical order. For example, you wouldn't want a submit button to come before a question.

- In Storyline, objects are read from top to bottom on the slide. If more than one object is at the same horizontal level, then the objects are read from left to right. Be sure to layout your page so that the objects can be read in a logical order.

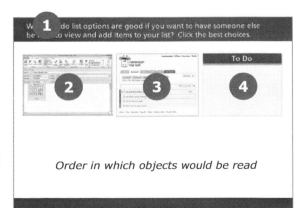

Order in which objects would be read

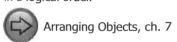 Arranging Objects, ch. 7

Creating a 508-Compliant Course (cont'd)

(m) When a web page requires that an applet, plug-in or other application be present on the client system to interpret page content, the page must provide a link to a plug-in or applet that complies with §1194.21(a) through (l).

If you are publishing to Flash, be sure to include links to the Adobe Flash Player BEFORE the student launches the course. (If they don't have the Flash player, they cannot access the first Storyline page with the link!) Also, be sure to provide links to Acrobat Reader and any other plug-ins required to view content.

 Publishing, ch. 15

(n) When electronic forms are designed to be completed on-line, the form shall allow people using assistive technology to access the information, field elements, and functionality required for completion and submission of the form, including all directions and cues.

- When creating forms, be sure to use only accessible options. See item (l) for question types that can be used. Individual buttons, check boxes, radio buttons, and data entry boxes added as interactive objects are accessible.

 Adding Interactive Objects, p. 116

(o) A method shall be provided that permits users to skip repetitive navigation links.

- If someone visits multiple web pages, they have to listen to (with a screen reader) and/or tab through (with keyboard navigation) all the main navigational elements each time they visit a new page. This standard requires that a link be provided that lets the user skip these items that appear on every page.

- If you include player elements such as a resources tab, glossary, or your own custom elements, these objects are considered repetitive and CANNOT be skipped. Therefore, they should not be used in a 508-compliant course. You can still use the **Notes** panel, because the content changes on every slide and is, therefore, not considered repetitive.

 Player, ch. 14

(p) When a timed response is required, the user shall be alerted and given sufficient time to indicate more time is required.

- Avoid using a timed test unless there is a job-specific reason for the timing. If you do use a timed test or add/build any content with a time limit, be sure to build in an extension system.

 Test Timer, p. 176

 BRIGHT IDEAS

- Accessibility can be defined in many different ways. The accessibility guidelines are subject to interpretation, and there is much debate about what makes a course usable and compliant. Therefore, it is extremely important that you carefully evaluate the standards and guidance provided by the government, accessibility groups, and your own organization (legal, HR, I.T., etc.) to determine what accessibility means for your organization.

- There is no substitute for thorough testing. Be sure to test your designs with accessibility devices to make sure they work as planned.

Notes

Index i

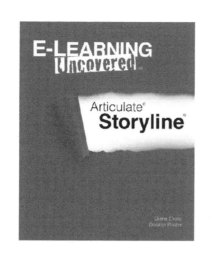

Visit the companion site at:

www.e-learninguncovered.com

Resources for Rapid Developers

1. Download free resources
2. Access practice files
3. Sign up for our blog
4. Ask about bulk purchases
5. Explore the other books in the series

Made in the USA
Charleston, SC
13 August 2013